SIX YEARS in BHUTAN

John Stedman

Design & formatting by Socciones Editoria Digitale

www.kindle-publishing-service.co.uk

CONTENTS

Map of the Indian sub-continent

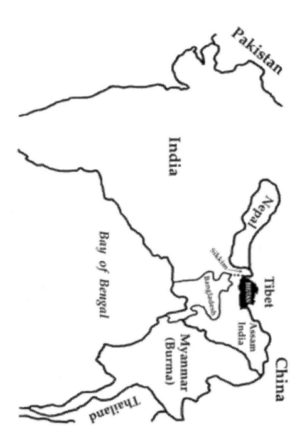

Map of Bhutan

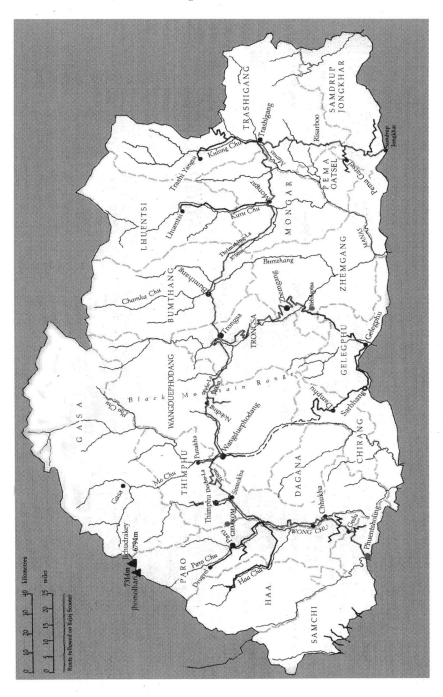

'To my wife Dorothy for her willing sacrifice and unwavering support and who kept me focused on the things that mattered.'

Introduction

In spring of 1984 Voluntary Service Overseas (VSO) confirmed my posting to Bhutan. When I told family, friends and work colleagues where I was going – their typical reactions were: "Bhutan, where's that?" "Bhutan, I've never heard of it!" "Where exactly in Africa is Bhutan?"

Very little was known about Bhutan as it was rarely if at all mentioned in the press or on TV or radio. I had only learnt of Bhutan's existence a year earlier during a visit to India. Naturally, as soon as the posting was confirmed I wanted to learn as much as possible about this remote and little known Kingdom; to prepare myself to live and work there for the next two years. I soon discovered that hardly anything was to be found in print. I did find a brief account by a Dr Peter Steele entitled *'Two and Two Halves to Bhutan'*, describing a journey with his wife and two children on horseback across Bhutan in 1967. This gave an intriguing glimpse into Bhutanese life and conveyed just how little the country had changed in several hundred years!

The **only** other source of information I could find, was an entry in the **Encyclopaedia Brittanica** which extended to just 4500 words, of which:-
1000 words were devoted to a description of Bhutan's position in the Himalaya and its topography;
1000 words described Bhutan's natural resources and economy – the opening sentence of which read "The natural resources of Bhutan have not been surveyed, and the precise extent of its agricultural, forest, mineral, and power resources is not yet known, an inventory of the country's natural resources is being taken ....";

500 words outlined Bhutan's known history; and another 500 the size, distribution and ethnic makeup of its population; – all of which though interesting was not of any immediate practical help.

Of the remaining 1500 words; 250 described Bhutan's transport system which consisted of just 120 miles of road used by 47 trucks and buses and its communication system consisting of a telephone link with India. One paragraph outlined the structure of Bhutan's government and another the justice system. Four sentences summed up all that was known of the existing health care in Bhutan.

<u>**One short paragraph**</u> was of any relevance to me: this was a brief summary of the Education system and stated - '**At present there are 105 schools with over 16,000 students.** *Lest the rapid spread of education without a matching expansion of employment opportunities should create an unemployment problem, emphasis is being gradually shifted to vocational education.*'

Encyclopaedia Britannica 1983

This information plus the little that the VSO Field Officer in Bangladesh was able to add, was all I knew of Bhutan when I left Britain to go to work there for the next two years.

<u>I was very much travelling into the unknown.</u>

Chapter 1

Journey into the Unknown

The apprehension felt in my stomach before boarding the tiny 18 seater aeroplane on the runway in Calcutta was not due to its small size. My sense of unease was because through the open door of the plane I could see a *steaming urn held only by a single strap, occupying the rear passenger seat*! It obviously contained very hot liquid, and I prayed that this tiny plane would not experience any violent turbulence as it flew through the remnants of the recent monsoon storm clouds.

I boarded with just six other passengers; including another teacher and the Field Director for Voluntary Service Overseas (VSO) based in Bangladesh, who was to see us settled into our new situations. We were handed a small white cardboard box containing the in-flight breakfast. Inside were two slices of bread and butter; a hard boiled egg still in its shell and a banana! We were not allocated seat numbers but there was no scramble to get a window seat - for they were all window seats! Welcome aboard the flight going to Paro, situated 6500 feet (2280m) up in the mountains of the tiny Himalayan Kingdom of Bhutan.

We lifted off from Calcutta just before sun-up in the relative cool of the early morning in the un-pressurised Dornier aircraft; one of only two that formed the entire fleet of the Bhutan State Airline - 'Druk Air' at that time. It was early September 1984 and this journey would mark a significant turning point in my life. Though I did not know it at the time, this was the start of six fascinating years spent in this little known and somewhat inaccessible country.

Situated at the eastern end of the Himalayan Mountain range the country of Bhutan is almost entirely mountainous from its southern border with India to its northern border with Tibet. It holds apart; or is sandwiched between; mighty China - the world's largest communist country and mighty India - the world's largest democracy. It is therefore both a 'Himalayan Kingdom' and a politically strategic 'buffer state'.

The plane climbed to a height of 8200 feet (2500m) and headed north over the flat plains of Bangladesh - still flooded from the recent monsoon rains. After about an hour steering carefully between enormous columns of cumulonimbus cloud that towered up way above our cruising altitude; thankfully without experiencing any dreaded air turbulence, we crossed the northern border of India into Bhutanese air space. Immediately, the flat cultivated open plains of India and Bangladesh gave way to the Himalayan foothills - a continuous range of mountains; forest clad to their summits with an almost unbroken carpet of green.

In the absence of cabin staff, the turbaned Sikh pilot appeared from behind a curtain that divided off the cockpit from the passenger cabin, to announce that we should help ourselves to coffee from the urn on the rear seat! Being nearest, I acted as steward and served my six fellow passengers, including two middle aged ladies toward the front of the plane. I noticed whilst the baggage was sitting on the tarmac waiting to be loaded, that their luggage was addressed c/o a leprosy hospital somewhere unpronounceable in Bhutan. They were complete strangers and I knew nothing about them or their destination but in that strange way in which lives are sometimes linked seemingly by chance, my work in Bhutan in years to come would be intertwined with theirs.

Flying between the mountains the plane followed the course of a steeply sided river valley leading north into the interior. In places the mountains on both sides of the plane seemed so close you might reach out and touch them. As we flew further north, small villages perched high on the mountainsides could be seen amid neat, steeply sloping fields. Then we were descending; banking sharply down between the mountains that threatened us on every side with the valley bottom rushing up to meet us. When the plane touched down, it juddered and bumped alarmingly along the very short airstrip to a rapid halt. We had landed at Paro airport, altitude 6500 feet (2280m) above sea level - the only air strip at this time in the Himalayan Kingdom.

So at last I'd arrived and it was immediately obvious that I'd entered a very different world to the one I'd left behind. Alighting from the aircraft on to Bhutanese soil for the very first time I had a sense of stepping into a uniquely different place; as if I'd journeyed back several centuries. There was a silence; broken only by the wind blowing up the valley mixed with the sounds of the few disembarking passengers; any noise being immediately wafted away and swallowed in the vastness of the mountains around.

We entered a tiny single storey terminal building - quite unlike any airport terminal I'd ever seen. It was beautifully and intricately painted on the outside in bright colours with snaking dragons and mysterious elaborate designs and its roof was formed of simple wooden shingles held down by stone boulders. The handful of passengers were processed with the utmost courtesy in about five minutes by Bhutan's 'immigration control' and after sorting our own luggage from the small pile in the corner; once our transport arrived we would be ready for the next stage of the journey. Meanwhile, we could relax outside under the clear deep blue sky and in the warm sunshine take stock of our new surroundings.

On the far side of the runway stretching up the hillside; stood ranks of tall poles with strips of cloth attached - prayer flags, fluttering in the breeze. Further up the Paro Valley beyond the end of the airstrip was a huge building, towering above the scattered houses in the fields around. It brought to mind in its architectural style pictures I had seen of the Potala Palace in Lhasa, Tibet. Massive gleaming white walls several stories high, tapered inwards slightly and highlighted the distinctive wide red ochre band that ran around the outside; parallel to and just below the roof. Standing up from within its interior stood a separate central tower crowned with a bright orange roof.

This impressive structure which dominated the whole valley I learnt later was a 'Dzong' and is the administrative, judicial and religious centre of Paro district. A Dzong of similar style is to be found in each of the seventeen districts of Bhutan; each one administered by a 'Dzongda', appointed by the King of Bhutan himself. The national language of Bhutan is 'Dzongkha', literally meaning the speech (kha) of the Dzong. Dzongkha is the official written language used throughout the whole of Bhutan but there are many local languages/dialects spoken within different valleys across the country.

4

Dotted about the valley were attractive wood-framed houses with very distinctive windows and doors. In appearance they looked somewhat like Elizabethan houses or Swiss chalets and they too featured wooden shingle roofs weighted down with boulders; obviously lifted from the bed of the river which flowed through the valley.

Our ongoing transport in the form of a jeep soon arrived; sent for us courtesy of the Education Department of His Majesty's Royal Government, to take us the next leg of our journey to Bhutan's capital - Thimphu. Thimphu is 30 or so miles (50 km) distant from Paro and at a breathless 8500 feet (2320m) above sea level.

This was of course my first experience of Bhutan's roads - definitely not for the faint hearted! The road from Paro to Thimphu is in fact one of the best in the country, running along the base of the mountains that flank it and lacking any of the sheer drops into oblivion which characterise so many roads elsewhere in Bhutan! Even so, we twisted and turned around every conceivable combination of bends: U bends, S bends, doglegs and hairpin bends; one following another in giddy succession; enough to make your head swim and stomach turn! After about two hours on this switchback, travelling through stunning mountain scenery and passing several small settlements of neat timber--framed houses surrounded by terraced fields; we finally reached our immediate destination – the capital Thimphu.

Thimphu is set in a broad fertile valley; with a wide but shallow river along its lower boundary lined with lush green willow trees. To the north, east and west; Thimphu is flanked by mountains. It could not be compared as a town to any in

Britain of my experience but was rather how I imagine a market town in mediaeval times to have been – a row of small shops stretching in a line along one side of a dusty main street. It had a raised stone pavement and water (and who knows what else) flowed in a channel beneath. The string of mostly one-storey, wood-framed, single- and double-fronted shops; were all built in the same traditional style, and like the airport terminal building were colourfully hand-painted with numerous intricate designs. Every one of the glassless shop fronts had a hinged shutter tied up over an inner counter where an amazing selection of merchandise was displayed. Behind the line of shops, more neat timber houses were scattered up the gently sloping valley floor toward the mountains beyond. On the other side of the main street stood a few, more modern multi-storey buildings, including the Central Bank, a Post Office and a Fire Station. Though these were obviously built of concrete; in an attempt to retain the traditional style of the wooden buildings, they also featured the same colourful decoration seen on all the traditional buildings.

During the few days of our stay in Thimphu we were generously provided with what the Bhutanese term *'fooding and lodging'* in a Government-owned hotel. We were received by the Director and other officials of the Education Department and given a grand tour of the capital - which took all of one afternoon! The offices of the Education Department were part of a complex of buildings on the northern edge of Thimphu adjacent to **Tashicho Dzong**; the Seat of the Royal Government where the King and His Council of Ministers are based. Tashicho Dzong was another most impressive building and looked in pristine condition; for this is where all visiting foreign dignitaries are received and where the National

6

Assembly or 'Tshogdu' was convened twice a year.

After three days in Thimphu adjusting gradually to its altitude, transport was provided to take me on to my final destination - the Kharbandi Technical College. The only technical college in Bhutan, and located 100 miles (170 km) from Thimphu to the south, near the border town of Phuentsholing.

Travelling there entailed another hair-raising journey, this time in a fairly ancient soft top jeep with open sides. We twisted and turned for over six hours on a narrow mountainside road and through heavy monsoon rain that constantly dripped through the jeep's canvas top. The mountains and valleys were cloaked in dense swirling cloud but every now and then, the veil of mist would pull back enough for me to glimpse a frightening drop of hundreds of feet from the road into a deep chasm below.

Eventually in the gathering twilight, we looked down under the clouds upon the border town of Phuentsholing a thousand feet below us. Beyond the town a river gleamed like a ribbon of silver curled across the flat open plain of India reaching into the distance. Thinley my Bhutanese driver stopped the jeep and pointed out the Kharbandi College complex below us; built on top of the very last hill in Bhutan; its buildings spaced neatly around open playing fields, and the whole campus surrounded by jungle extending down the hillside toward the edge of the town beneath.

Our journey south had brought us again almost to sea level and now I was faced with a different kind of acclimatisation! There were so many unanswered questions about Kharbandi

College that I must have been wondering as I looked down on it for the first time; just how things were going to work out over the next two years. I was the first teacher to be appointed here to work for the Royal Government arranged through VSO. Practically nothing was known about my living conditions or the teaching I would be expected to undertake. In Britain I'd taught Mathematics and Engineering Drawing and Design for some twenty years, in a large well-equipped Engineering Department of a college in Kent; but I'd been warned at interview that I might be expected to teach other subjects here at Kharbandi; but just what, was more than just a trifle hazy!

There were so many other unanswered questions, beside what subjects I might be asked to teach. Would I be living on campus? What would my living quarters be like? Was there an electricity supply? What would the other staff be like and how would they react to my appointment? What teaching resources were there? What books were available – if any? What would my hours and duties be? But because I was the first to be appointed to Kharbandi and one of the first teachers from Britain to enter this little known Kingdom of Bhutan; VSO was unable to give definitive answers to many of my questions.

One fact that VSO was aware of about Bhutan was the harsh winter conditions and freezing temperatures experienced in its capital Thimphu. So I was considerately equipped with a warm duck down jacket and a good quality, four seasons, duck down sleeping bag. But such are the variations of climate in Bhutan, that Kharbandi turned out to be in a *subtropical* region; where the temperature in summer reaches 100*F with nearly 100 per cent humidity! Down here on the

Indian border at no time of the year did the temperature remotely approach zero!

I had real difficulty deciding what I should take to get me through my two-*year* assignment because officially I had the same 20Kg luggage allowance that you would have for a two *week* holiday to the Mediterranean! After prolonged bargaining and even pleading at the British Airways check-in desk at Heathrow, I succeeded in stretching this to 30 Kg. Even then I was forced under the threat of parting with some of my precious traveller's cheques (taken for emergency evacuation use only) to pay for excess baggage charges; to off-load some items to a friend who had come to see me off - to bring the weight down to the decreed 30 kg final, *absolutely* final, *definitely* final - limit.

Just the books I imagined I might require accounted for a significant part of the weight allowance. Beside a good general Maths textbook and two on Engineering Drawing and Design; I also took a thick, small print 'Engineers Handbook' packed with information on all manner of engineering topics that might just get me out of a fix should I be asked to teach a subject I had never taught before! One more vital book I was urged to take by VSO, was *'Where There is No Doctor'*; a wide ranging guide on what measures one can take if you fall ill or meet with an accident in a place where there's no professional medical assistance! It brought home to me that I was not to expect the kind of health care in Bhutan, that you get from Britain's National Health Service - which until now like most other British citizens, I had taken somewhat for granted.

A small battery operated short-wave radio on which I could listen to the BBC World Service; together with rechargeable batteries and a solar-powered battery charger seemed essential; living in such an isolated place and being the only non-Asian on the staff. Then I had included thick warm clothing and the four season's sleeping bag in preparation for the very cold climate (which of course turned out to be quite hot); sufficient toothpaste and shaving cream which used sparingly might last me the two years; as well as a few personal items - such as my address book, a very small photo album, writing materials and a Bible. It was just as well weight-wise that I had excluded the complete works of Shakespeare in travelling to my particular 'Desert Island'! As I hoped to do some trekking I wore walking boots on the flight to save weight! Lastly, being a keen photographer; I took a 35mm SLR camera plus lenses and an ample bulk supply of film and a film loader; carried on board as hand baggage in the largest case permitted that would fit under the seat. Fortunately, in 1984 this 7 kg was not counted as part of my luggage allowance!

So after many months of planning and preparation I had finally arrived safely, along with my luggage; as prepared (or unprepared depending on how you looked at it) as I could be, to teach at Kharbandi Technical College. In spite of my many years of experience in teaching, now that I had actually arrived I felt some apprehension about what I might be faced with.

That this initial venture into the unknown would eventually lead to my spending *six years in Bhutan,* or that Kharbandi would be my home for any longer than my then two-year contract with VSO; I didn't have the slightest inkling! Nor that teaching here would eventually lead me to undertake the most worthwhile but at the same time most demanding challenge of my whole working life; in an even more remote part of this isolated and other world. Six challenging and rewarding years - not in material gain but in an enriching encounter with a unique and antique land. Six years in a country as yet largely unexposed to, or spoiled by, the outside world. Six years among a sophisticated people but one whose way of life and thinking had hardly changed since mediaeval times. In 1984: Bhutan was only just beginning to come to terms with being part of the wider world community and only just beginning to emerge from its self-imposed isolation of centuries; to embark on a process of integration with the world outside its borders. A country which not many years before, had only known the wheel as an instrument of prayer and was to yet discover that turned on its side it could be used to great effect for transport!

I was about to discover the challenges that a country such as Bhutan presents to anyone from the developed world; who in most any and every situation is used to having all manner of back-up services they can call on, as and when needed. The help of the police, fire and ambulance services in an emergency; breakdown assistance from the AA or RAC when in trouble on the road; the help of a technician, secretary or librarian at school or college; or an electrician or plumber to sort out a problem at home. Here in Bhutan no such services existed!

I was also about to discover how limited my past life experience had been; having lived and worked up to this point in my life, in a wholly westernised, consumer orientated, materialistic, time conscious, and traditionally Christian country - without giving too much thought to what difference this made. Now my limited outlook and philosophy of life up to this point was about to be revealed and challenged; for I now found myself isolated in an entirely Asian, subsistent, non-materialistic, almost timeless and very Buddhist society.

They say life begins at forty - well mine at forty-five was about to be pealed back to the basics here in the **'Thunder Dragon Kingdom'** or **'Druk Yul'** as the Bhutanese call it, and to be put to the test in ways that no amount of formal qualifications or previous work experience could ever have prepared me for. In this antique land my preconceptions were about to be confronted and my wider education about to begin!

Chapter 2

A Different Way of Life

At Kharbandi College the majority of staff was resident on campus in family quarters, and dormitory accommodation housed the 300 plus male students. On arrival, my allotted accommodation turned out to be a former Jesuit priest's 'cell'! It was located above the classrooms and was a sparsely furnished concrete room about 5 paces x 3, with a small cooking area off the back; together with toilet and shower room. Though small, it was perfectly adequate for my needs and it included what I soon came to realise was a luxury for Bhutan - a western style pedestal toilet. However, I quickly discovered that one of the biggest frustrations of my new life was to be the water supply - when there was one that is. This was routed from a header tank and came over the top of the roof of the building in a bare un-lagged pipe. It meant that in the cooler 'winter' months when warm water would have been nice, it was stone cold! In the very hot sticky summer months when a cold shower would have brought some relief, it came out of the tap almost too hot to bear!

Our water supply was piped from a mountain stream some distance away in the hills above the college, into a very large prefabricated metal holding tank, from which it was distributed to all the various buildings. The water system had been installed by the Jesuit priests who apparently were responsible for founding and building the college. It had been more than adequate for the college's requirements; until that is, since its installation, other users had tapped into the college's supply rather than find an alternative of their own. 'Our' water was now also piped to a government-owned hotel nearby - for prestigious visitors coming into Bhutan via India and fully expecting no doubt a good water supply in their bathrooms; a royal palace to which the King's ageing grandmother along with her retinue of servants came to stay from Paro in the winter months when temperatures were much kinder down here and who most definitely had to have a reliable water supply; and last but not least, it was shared by a cottage hospital down on the edge of the nearby town - also needing a plenteous supply to maintain any basic level of hygiene. All these additional demands made on the original college water system, had altogether proved just too much!

Each year during the hot dry summer before the monsoon arrived, the college ran short of water! Its needs it seemed, were now regarded as less important that those of the other 'parasitic' consumers. With little water either to wash with or to wash clothes in, coupled with the fact that often there was no electricity either to operate the ceiling fans; the classroom would noticeably hum during the hottest weather, with forty sweaty unwashed young men in the class, not to mention their teacher! To cap it all, the whole water system was operated by a labourer who was drunk as often as he was sober. I was convinced that much of the time he had no idea whether he was opening or closing the stopcocks that controlled and dispatched the water to one or other of its consumers!

Years later, looking back on this unsatisfactory situation and the obvious deficiencies of the college water supply system and how it had been plagiarised and mismanaged; my frustrating experience was to be put to good use when faced with finding a solution for a very similar situation elsewhere in Bhutan.

Dawa Gyaltshen

The day after I arrived at Kharbandi it was suggested by the Acting Principal, that until I found out what food was available and where to shop for my needs I might find it easier to 'mess' with a Mr Sharma; a friendly if enigmatic single Indian staff member of about my own age. The suggestion was well intentioned but proved to be an arrangement that worked better in theory than in practice. Mr Sharma was a high caste Indian and a strict vegetarian. His diet excluded not only meat but fish and eggs as well and seemed to consist of rice in large quantities; together with dhal, nuts and fruit. It was definitely not my idea of an enjoyable diet and the arrangement only lasted a couple of weeks, by which time I felt I'd eaten enough rice to last me a lifetime!

To help and assist with my initial settling in to living and

Pema Gyeltshen

teaching at Kharbandi, I was put under the care of two senior Bhutanese members of staff; Dawa Gyaltshen and Pema Gyeltshen. With the greatest courtesy, tact and thoughtfulness imaginable, they took me under their wing in all matters - personal, professional and cultural. They were truly the best ambassadors their country could have wished for and I found their willing assistance and friendship invaluable in helping me overcome problems and difficulties; especially in the first few months while I was settling down and adjusting to my new life. Nothing was too much trouble for them. They were always on hand to help - and gave it with genuine pleasure, a smile and words of encouragement. Their care extended to offering hospitality and welcoming me into their homes and their families and more often than not after teaching was over for the day, I would be invited for a cup of tea and a chat at Dawa's or Pema's. I was to get to know and value them both as true and trusted friends throughout my six years in Bhutan.

On my first few visits to the homes of staff for a 'cup of tea' I was given 'suja'- the standard Bhutanese tea which tasted radically different to any tea I'd been used to! To make suja, tea is chipped from a solid block and boiled in water. Butter and salt are then added and the mixture churned together in a bamboo cylinder. It tastes more like salty soup than your English 'cuppa' and took some getting used to. It was somewhat disconcerting when before you had forced down all of the bowl of greasy suja, it was topped up again by your host! It was only much later that I learned it's customary for the host to top up a guests bowl three times; and it was expected of me as a guest to politely receive three refills! In time, I learnt to sip my suja *very slowly* and so restrict the size of refills to an absolute minimum without causing offence. This greasy, salty tea is an acquired taste and one that I never really grew to embrace!

Living in such a very different culture to my own, it was easy to jump to the wrong conclusions based on my own cultural background and conditioning. My erroneous logic might subsequently prove to be not only incorrect but embarrassingly so! However, the Bhutanese are generally too polite to correct errant behaviour; even when according to their customs your actions might seem discourteous or even outrageous! For example - not being the world's keenest cook and as my cooking facilities were rather more primitive than I'd been used to; in the first few months I was grateful to accept the numerous kind invitations to eat with staff members and their families - both Bhutanese and Indian. Their main meal of the day is taken in the evening and having been told they normally ate around eight, I politely arrived just beforehand. The meal then seemed to take an inordinate time to reach the table and would invariably be served around nine; by which time I was ravenously hungry and inwardly speculating as to what could have caused the long delay? When at last we'd finished eating I would sit on afterwards and chat politely until ten or ten thirty before saying good night and retiring to my quarters.

This pattern of behaviour before and after my meals out, I repeated several times in different homes without a second thought. Two or three months probably passed, during which time the staff room could well have been buzzing with comment - had I been able to understand Dzongkha; before I was made aware of the very different etiquette in Bhutan! Their custom is for a guest to arrive an hour or so *before* a meal and to chat with their host while the food is being prepared and until the wife then serves the food. After eating, a guest is expected to leave almost immediately, to allow the wife to eat and the family to then retire to bed! Unwittingly, not only had I kept everyone waiting prior to the meal, as the lady of the house would not dream of starting to cook before their guest arrived; I had also kept the family up afterwards well past their bed time! Eventually, when I suppose they knew me well enough; someone - probably Pema or Dawa, broke with tradition and no doubt ever so tactfully told me what the accepted norm was, when invited to an Asian home for an evening meal! In time I also learned that when eating with a Bhutanese family it is polite to refuse a second helping no less than three times before finally accepting; likewise, whenever you're entertaining Bhutanese guests, it is worth remembering that according to their custom, good manners requires them to refuse more food three times and only then to accept your offer of a further helping!

When you ate with a Bhutanese family there was often a dish containing raw chillies and salt on the table, to munch on before the main dish is served! The Bhutanese are very fond of chillies and the hotter they are the more they like them! They did not appreciate of course that the eating of burning hot raw chillies, did not form a part of my normal diet! The main staple food in Bhutan is rice which is eaten in some quantity and this is often served with chillies, or sometimes with sliced potato mixed with a local cheese or '*datsi*' which is very nice and for my taste anyway much preferred to chillies. There is a particular kind of rice grown in Bhutan known as 'red' rice, which is especially tasty.

I celebrated my forty fifth birthday within a month of arrival; this made me one of the oldest staff members at Kharbandi.

The Asians in general and the Bhutanese in particular treat their elders with special respect. Even in their everyday address or greeting this veneration of ones' elders would be shown by adding *'la'* - a mark of respect, to the end of a sentence; even when speaking in English. So I would be greeted for example not with 'Good morning' but with 'Good morning *la*!' There is actually an honorific form of the national language 'Dzongkha' that is always used by Bhutanese to address those of higher rank in society. My being regarded as of a 'venerable' age also meant, that any staff member younger than me, or junior in position (which included most of the staff) would be most reluctant to correct any errant behaviour on my part.

Another cultural frustration was that Bhutanese are, generally speaking, very reluctant to say 'no' to anything in case they give offence. This is most confusing to a Western way of thinking, as it makes it difficult if not impossible for a 'Westerner' to determine whether the answer to a request is genuinely 'yes', or really 'no'! On a number of occasions this particular quirk of Bhutanese culture was to have somewhat serious repercussions especially during the building project for which I was responsible, later on in Bhutan.

There was also the whole minefield of Bhutanese names and relationships. At first I foolishly reasoned that students with a shared second name of say Dorji; (which is very common and the equivalent, so I first assumed, of being called Smith or Jones in Britain); might indicate in a population as small as Bhutan's (less than one million) if coming from the same village; that two such individual's were possibly related to one other! I eventually discovered that apart from the King inherited family names are rarely owned in Bhutan - except that is by the people of Nepali origin living in the south of the country, who being mainly Hindu had a family caste name. In the rest of Bhutan where Tibetan Buddhism is the religion of the vast majority, a child is given its name not by or from its parents, but by the Buddhist monk or lama. One member of staff, whose first name was Sangey, told me he had five brothers; all of whom had been given the same name Sangey by the lama! Pity their poor mother! To confuse matters further, girls share many of the same names as boys! As I was teaching in an all-male establishment I never did find out how the system of names actually worked! It seems however, that the name given to a girl is recognisably different - recognisable to a Bhutanese that is; and that many female names tend to end in 'om' meaning milk - very logical once you've cracked the code! All Bhutanese names have religious as well as natural meanings. For example, Sangey means 'the Buddha', Dawa means 'sun', Pema is 'lotus'.

With such duplication of names and in the absence of any inherited family surname; I really don't know how the government will ever manage to administer a tax system or keep a reliable register of the populace! As there was no marriage ceremony in Bhutan and polygamy, polyandry (more than one husband) as well as monogamy were all to be found there, I think any attempt to keep an accurate official register of the population would be rendered virtually impossible!

Every student seemed to have a multitude of 'cousin brothers' - a term used for any male relative apart that is from a brother! Yet no matter how tenuous a relationship might be, a Bhutanese seemed to always know when someone was related to them and was willing to provide 'fooding and lodging' for even the most distantly related individual for however long a time it was needed; whenever required and without prior notice.

Living and working in such a different culture and being so isolated from contact with other westerners was not always easy. For the first sixteen months not only was I the only non-Asian on the staff but also in the whole district. Although my Bhutanese colleagues could not have done more to make me feel welcome, I nevertheless felt quite isolated at times. It was important to sometimes take myself off or lock myself in where I would not be disturbed, and spend some time in quiet contemplation and private devotion to put my life in perspective. This was especially true as I became aware of certain things in the College that were not ethical and needed to be challenged. The saying about 'changing those things that can be changed and leaving alone those that cannot and having the wisdom to know the difference,' could not have been more apt.

Unbeknown to me when I first arrived; the Jesuit priests who had founded and built the college as a 'Don Bosco' School had been ousted from the country about three years before I was appointed on a charge of proselytising - which was forbidden in Bhutan. A charge made against them, so I came to understand, by a small number of the Bhutanese staff who were still employed there. This explained why VSO had questioned me at some length at my selection interview, as to how I as a practising Christian thought I would be able to work alongside those of other faiths. Sadly, since the priests' demise and departure and in the absence of any proper auditory control, some college resources were now being misappropriated. These practices were a considerable hindrance to the harmonious working relationship that otherwise existed but as much as I abhorred what was obviously detrimental to the students' welfare, in the main I could do nothing about them. I must add that during my six years in Bhutan I found the vast majority of the Bhutanese people to be extremely honest and trustworthy and any form of corruption was in my experience rare.

Writing or receiving letters did not form part of the everyday life of the average Bhutanese - a consequence perhaps of their living in isolation from the rest of the world for so many centuries! Naturally to receive mail from home was an important part of life for me when living in such an isolated situation. I looked forward enormously to letters, especially from my son at university and my daughter then in her final year of nurse training; as well as from close friends who kindly wrote keeping me in touch with home. Mail was delivered to the college office daily, Monday to Saturday, but I soon discovered the office staff had no idea of how important it was that a letter having already taken three weeks or more to reach Bhutan should be passed on without further delay. Letters might well lie in the office under a pile of paper for the weekend or longer before they were eventually uncovered and passed on.

I could also tell that my letters had invariably been opened somewhere along their route before reaching me; as the letter was often clumsily glued into the flap of the envelope by mistake when it had been resealed. I think this probably happened in India rather than Bhutan, as all my mail had to pass through India and they kept a careful eye on foreigners working in Bhutan. The advent of e-mail, satellite communication and the use of mobile phones must now make such surveillance almost impossible. The British postal service wasn't sure either on which continent Bhutan was situated; some Christmas cards arrived for me three months late having travelled via Africa - just in time for Easter!

There was a telephone in the college office and you always knew when it was in use. Even for a local call, to make oneself heard to the person at the other end it was necessary to shout down the mouthpiece at the top of one's voice. The actual line was routed via a very ancient Indian telephone exchange in Phuentsholing, housing banks of noisy mechanical tumblers; and thence by wire strung pole to pole and mostly covered in creeper the 100 miles or so to Thimphu. I marvelled that the system worked at all! To telephone Britain, a journey to Thimphu was necessary as it was not possible to make international calls from Phuentsholing. I did this once to give my daughter a surprise on her birthday and I had to make my call from the main telephone Exchange in Thimphu. Getting the call through to London took virtually the whole night! Bhutan time is five hours ahead of GMT and whilst I camped down inside the Exchange on a mattress; the telephonist tried manfully to get a line for me by the only route then open to London which was via Delhi. Eventually, after several hours of frustration and full marks for persistence; several hours past midnight Bhutan time but at 10pm GMT, the operator finally succeeded in connecting me and I was able to wish her a happy birthday just before it ended! Today there is a direct satellite link from Thimphu to anywhere in the world and I am told that even calls to neighbouring India, go via London!

The BBC World Service was my main window on the world and I tuned in daily to keep abreast of news and current affairs. I was also able to receive very loud and clear, Radio Moscow and the Voice of America, on my short-wave portable. I constantly gave thanks for the objective and balanced news coverage of the BBC - largely free of the political claptrap peddled by the other two. I became convinced of the enormous prestige and value to Britain of the BBC World Service in maintaining such a quality, relatively unbiased, broadcasting service. It was a sad day indeed in my opinion, when short-sighted politicians decided that the BBC World Service was costing too much and must be cut back to make some minimal financial saving.

Of course, a television was not included among my scant furnishings and in any case, television was banned until as recently as 1998. During my time there, even receiving programmes broadcast from nearby India or Bangladesh or elsewhere; was officially illegal. However, our students had a legal way around this unwelcome restriction imposed on their enjoyment of TV. Bhutanese are quite legitimately and freely allowed to cross the border with India; which runs right through the middle of the town of Phuentsholing. So as always, some enterprising Indian businessmen had seized their opportunity and opened 'video houses'; in India but strategically sited along the open border with Bhutan! The only time students were permitted to leave the campus was a Sunday afternoon, when there was a mass exodus down to Phuentsholing. Bearing in mind they were all virile young males; surprisingly, the irresistible attraction was not in meeting up with girls nor was it to buy food to supplement the college rations - it was television! You had only to go along the border at three thirty on a Sunday afternoon, to see many of our students coming out of the improvised galvanised iron sheds that passed as 'video houses', having enjoyed their TV entertainment for the week.

Later on during my time at Kharbandi a colour television set appeared on campus - part of a technical aid package from a western donor who shall be nameless! I have no idea how it was learned that every Friday night we could receive recorded full coverage of a top league UK football match, re-broadcast from Bangladesh! The whole male college population (including myself), numbering about 320 or so; crammed into a small room about twice the size of a domestic lounge, to watch a match that had been played several weeks earlier and was now re-broadcast on Bangladeshi TV - complete with some very western adverts at half time! I have never, ever, seen so many bodies squashed into such a small space; as all 300+ males crammed themselves in layers – lying, sitting, standing and balanced on benches at the back; to watch an out-of -date football match (plus the strange totally inappropriate foreign adverts during half time) on one modest TV set! I'm sure it must qualify for an entry into the Guinness Book of Records!

I might have been deprived of the 'telly' for most of the time but life at Kharbandi did have its compensations. For anyone interested in astronomy the night sky was fabulously clear for most of the year and viewing conditions just about perfect; Kharbandi, as well as being elevated high above the plain of India was surrounded by forest, which stabilises the atmosphere. As there were few artificial lights around, the stars shone night after night with a clarity and brightness only experienced very occasionally in remote parts of Britain. In 1970 I had built a Newtonian reflecting telescope with an eight-and-a half-inch diameter mirror. The main tube of this telescope was about six-foot long so it was much too large to transport to Bhutan! When I saw the amazingly clear night sky at Kharbandi, I thought it would be a great project to build the first telescope in Bhutan. Kind friends of mine in Tonbridge in December of 1985 purchased and sent out to me a four-inch diameter parabolic telescope mirror, plus a suitable eyepiece. So with the use of the college workshop facilities I was able to make a reasonably powerful telescope. The main tube was finished and its optics installed just in time to witness a total eclipse of the moon.

Whenever there is a lunar eclipse in Bhutan their belief is that the moon is being eaten by a dragon! To prevent this tragedy, people come out of doors and bang together any objects they can lay hold of to create a din and so frighten the dragon away! Of course this strategy always proves successful! On the night of the particular eclipse the seeing conditions were perfect and with the telescope supported on a temporary mount it was possible for us to observe the event. The full lunar eclipse lasted quite a long time and a queue of students and staff waited to get their first glimpse of the moon through an astronomical telescope. The Earth's shadow gradually advanced across the face of the moon until it was completely covered and typically appeared as a copper coloured disc. I particularly remember one of the staff after peering intently into the eyepiece, said to me rather tellingly with a touch of wonder in his voice; 'O yes, I can see _now_ that it _really is_ a shadow!' Later on we were able to view the more spectacular planets - to see the rings of Saturn; and the major moons, equatorial bands and the Great Red Spot on Jupiter; as well as resolve the Milky Way into its countless millions of individual stars.
The Bhutanese know very well when eclipses of the moon will occur as these are accurately predicted by their Buddhist

astrologers who devise the calendar used in Bhutan. This calendar based on the lunar cycle is a fascinating document; as certain days in each month are held to be 'auspicious' and others 'inauspicious'. The 8th, 15th (full moon) and last day's are always regarded as auspicious. Such predictions are taken very seriously, so much so that if a particular day is deemed to be 'inauspicious' in that month, it may be left off the calendar altogether! On the other hand, should a day be deemed to be 'auspicious' it will often be repeated twice over in that month. Occasionally I believe, a complete lunar month of thirty days will be declared as 'auspicious' and so be duplicated on the calendar!

Even educated Bhutanese could be influenced directly or indirectly by such things. A very high-ranking official in the Education Department once confided to me that he was reluctant to travel on a Friday; stressing that this was not because he personally any longer believed that Friday was an inauspicious day for travel as was generally thought; but because his mother believed it, and in order to please her he never travelled on Fridays! Not being familiar with either the Bhutanese calendar or culture during my early months living at Kharbandi I was taken by surprise on several occasions; discovering only when it actually arrived, that what I expected to be a normal working day was in fact a public religious holiday. For example, the fourth day of the sixth month was a public holiday to commemorate when Buddha first preached his religious principles. 'Blessed Rainy Day' was celebrated on the 22nd of September as marking the end of the monsoon. There seemed to be an amazing number of such one-day holidays! In Thimphu the first day each year that it snowed was an official public holiday but down here in the sub-tropical south we were denied this day off as it never snowed!

It was rather infuriating to learn of a public holiday at the last minute or on the morning of the actual day, when it was far too late for me to make arrangements to take advantage of the extra day off to get away from campus for a break. The rest of the staff had their families with them and so enjoyed a family day; whereas I was left with little alternative but to make the best of a bad job and use my unexpected break from teaching to catch up on domestic chores and letter writing, etc...

Staff members and their wives made at least one weekly trip down to Phuentsholing, four kilometres away, to buy food and anything else they might need. Each Saturday after lunch when there were no classes and our students were employed in duties around the campus, the vintage college bus was provided for this shopping excursion. This was a staff social event and the only time when many of the families left the college campus! Being a border town, in Phuentsholing it was possible to purchase a surprising selection of goods. At the **'Tashi'** 'emporium' you could buy 'milk bread', biscuits, tinned tuna fish, dried mushrooms, Indian made corn flakes (which tasted like cardboard) and surprisingly - very good 'Druk' orange marmalade. To my amazement Tashi stores even had a photographer's where I could purchase Kodak roll film and get negative colour film developed and printed. Soon I became acquainted with its Indian proprietor, who was most obliging when he discovered I was based at Kharbandi and a keen photographer to boot, so a most promising customer.

Such luxuries and facilities were only to be found in Bhutan's border towns, so I counted myself fortunate indeed to have access to such goods and services. Phuentsholing had a daily open-air market where a wide selection of fruit and vegetable was available; as well as meat, poultry and fish, all brought in from India. You had to ignore the vast swarm of flies on the meat and fish and the general lack of hygiene and just make sure that any harmful bacteria was well and truly killed off during cooking. Eggs were available but were very anaemic looking - the yokes being a washed out pale yellow. When you purchased eggs the vendor examined them one at a time held in front of an electric light bulb - I assume to ensure there was no embryo chick inside!

My one treat each week during the Saturday shopping trip, was to have lunch out at an Indian run establishment called the 'Kunga Hotel' - a cheap but clean restaurant come lodging house. Here I enjoyed a weekly meal of Chinese style sweet and sour chicken with egg fried rice and a glass of refrigerated mango juice, all for just a few rupees! As I was officially employed by the Education Department of the Royal Government I was paid the same as my Bhutanese colleagues - the then princely sum of £30 per month; paid in the national currency of Bhutan, the Ngultrum – equivalent in value to one Indian rupee. In the Bhutanese currency 100 *chetrum*'s = one *ngultrum*. My accommodation was provided rent free as part of the deal. It was possible to live on this salary and have my one meal out a week but there was little cash left each month.

Apart from Saturday when I lunched out, I made it a principle that no matter how little I might feel like cooking (which was especially so during the hot and humid summer months) I would always force myself to cook one decent meal per day. In time my kitchen was reasonably equipped with a two ring gas hob that worked from bottled gas; an Indian-made pressure cooker (that only blew its gasket once); a couple of saucepans and a few kitchen utensils - all obtained in Phuentsholing. Later on when the need became apparent VSO paid for me to get a small refrigerator - a tremendous help in preventing food from going off during the very hot summer months. My kitchen had water on tap - some of the time! All in all, I was well provided for by Bhutanese standards and compared to VSO primary school teachers working in remote villages; many having to manage without electricity, piped water, or a proper toilet and having to walk miles for food and other essential supplies - I was in the lap of luxury!

Though I never skimped on food, I had no worry about putting on weight. During the hottest months if I walked down to the market for groceries, by the time I climbed back up to Kharbandi I would be soaked in perspiration. I often wondered if the energy loss in making the trip exceeded the calorific value of the food I had managed to carry back! When I returned to Britain after two years, my weight had dropped by 13 Kg that's more than two stone 'in old money'!

To counter the bacteria that proliferate in the sub-tropical heat I usually cooked my meals in a pressure cooker, knowing that the 120 *C at which it operates would kill off all harmful bugs in the process. It also conserved the precious Calor gas by substantially shortening the cooking time. Alternatively, I would deep fry fish - in batter (how else) – served together with chipped potatoes! A good supply of fish was to be had from the local market and though the different types available were all quite unknown to me, I soon got to learn which tasted most like cod or plaice! Of course I had to gut and clean the fish which posed a bit of a problem when there was no water! As I had always done, I removed and discarded the fish heads before frying but after some time my Asian neighbours discovered this and expressed incredulity that I was throwing away the best part of the fish. Thereafter I was able to foster good international relations by donating the fish heads to my Indian neighbours.

When fresh mangoes came into season and first appeared in the market, my Asian neighbours became very excited. At first I couldn't understand their passion but soon grew to love this most succulent fruit. My Bhutanese neighbours also introduced me to a food called 'fern cross' - a vegetable which you could purchase at a certain time of year for just a few rupees. It looked rather like the curly head of bracken when it first breaks through the ground, but since bracken is poisonous I knew it had to be some kind of fern. Cooked in a knob of butter for just a few minutes, 'fern cross' was the most delicious vegetable. Fresh garden peas were also obtainable for a short time of the year and my neighbours taught me not to discard the pea pods but to peel away their inner lining and cook the pods along with the peas – when they became perfectly edible! Little was wasted - which was just as well as there was no refuse collection service.

The average Bhutanese possessed very little in the way of worldly goods so they really valued what little they had. Any containers which could be put to further use such as empty tins, bottles, etc., were saved and utilised. The small amount of household waste that could not be recycled was squashed flat and buried in a deep hole in the ground; so 'fly-tipped' waste was never seen. My students would not dream for a moment of scrapping even a partly used piece of paper and would carefully use every inch of both sides of every page.

Nothing was wasted! Though people had so little they were most generous in sharing what little they had - even with a complete stranger like me.

As Kharbandi is so near to the border at Phuentsholing, the main gateway for visitors coming and going via Bagdogra in India; I was sometimes asked to provide overnight accommodation to folk as they passed through. It was a pleasure to do this as it meant company to chat with and a chance to learn more about the varied development project's they were involved in; as by no means all of my overnight visitors were teachers with VSO. Andrew, one of my guests, was a dietician working on an interesting project to introduce iodised salt into the general diet across Bhutan in place of the salt then being used. The purpose of this project was to reduce the widespread problem of goitres. Because Bhutan is so far from the sea there is a general deficiency in the vital element iodine - a deficiency that causes goitres to form. People with the unsightly neck swelling typical of goitre sufferers, were a common sight.

Cooking the evening meal for such occasional guests was the only down side. The way round this was to provide a supper of good British fare - Fish and Chips! It was the one dish certain to be appreciated by anyone working in the interior of Bhutan where it was almost impossible to obtain fish - unless you caught it yourself. One Swiss couple who had been working for several years in central Bhutan with the Swiss development agency 'Helvetas,' stayed a night with me on their way home. To express their thanks for B & B and their Fish and Chip supper, they presented me with a superb and very useful Swiss army penknife before leaving next morning - a gift that I still treasure.

Providing hospitality also forged useful links with people working in different locations across Bhutan; who were equally happy to reciprocate in offering you a meal and a bed for the night and this was to prove useful on my travels across country.

Chapter 3

Living Close to Nature

The weather at Kharbandi varied from hot to very hot and from dry to 100% humidity and very, very wet! The most pleasant period was during the so-called winter. Though we never experienced frost; first thing in the morning there could be a definite chill in the air but throughout the rest of the day it would be nicely cool and dry. As the year progressed and the monsoon came closer, so the temperatures climbed steadily up towards 100* Fahrenheit; when it became increasingly difficult to work, difficult to eat, and especially difficult to sleep - as the perspiration poured out of you day and night. To cap it all, as the water ran short it also became difficult to wash!

It was at this time of the year that the insect population noticeably proliferated! Our natural instinctive reaction to insects is to either draw back from them, or swipe them before they have a chance to bite us – not without some justification. Yet being the most numerous kind of life on our planet their variety and ingenuity is boundless and they never ceased to intrigue me. My kitchen was furnished with a metal-topped wooden table the legs of which were peppered with mysterious holes, as if a giant-sized wood worm had had a go at it. When the hot summer arrived, the origin of these holes was revealed; when from time to time I would see a wasp-like creature fly in through the open window on regular sorties - with the corpse of an insect slung below; which it would then proceed to stuff into one of the holes in a leg of my table! The kitchen table obviously served as a nursery for this creature's grubs where they were being nurtured until ready to wing their way off! Not one's idea of kitchen hygiene but it made the chore of cooking much more interesting!

Also during the hottest months, the cockroach numbers increased considerably, especially in the kitchen. They would seldom be seen by day unless I pulled out the refrigerator or rummaged in the back of a cupboard but at night they ventured out of hiding to forage for any tiny morsels, such as a crumb of bread or a grain of sugar that may have been spilt. I always wore 'flip-flops' on my feet when out of bed at night, as you would often crunch a marauding cockroach underfoot in the darkness on your way to the toilet!

Throughout the summer the mosquitoes became numerous and most troublesome. In the evening it was necessary to keep your arms covered and at night to sleep under a mosquito net. Particularly after dark you would hear their distinctive buzzing as one tried to alight on your neck or ear. They are very persistent in their endeavours to obtain your lifeblood, as the protein it contains is vital to enable the female mosquito to breed. Though I slept under a net and carefully tucked it in all round under the mattress to keep out intruders, they still managed to get at me. Their infra-red vision detects the heat from your body, so when you turn over in your sleep and happen to touch the net they will be gathered waiting their chance to access your precious protein. The white-washed wall beside my bed was plastered in small red blotches where I had managed to swat offending mos'ies already full of my blood. At least these would not procreate and increase the mosquito population any further! It seemed no matter what measures you took to combat mosquitoes; fitting inner frames of mosquito netting at the windows and doors; sleeping under a protective net; using special slow burning chemical coils in the bedroom at night; as well as the spraying of DDT by diligent government employees, all around the buildings, including down the face of the chalkboards in the classrooms; some mosquitoes would still make it through all these defences!

What with the heat, the humidity and the mosquitoes, sleep at this time of the year was very difficult. Without the luxury of air conditioning I would lay on top of my mattress with a ceiling fan going at full speed directly over me to deter the mosquitoes and at the very least circulate the hot air and make it *'feel'* more comfortable.

Just before the onset of the monsoon, fireflies made their appearance. I had seen glow-worms in the Devon and Kent countryside but glow-worms hardly compare with the magical charm of these tiny glowing creatures as they wing through the tropical night with their light flashing to attract a mate. One evening when travelling on the road below Kharbandi with my colleague Dawa, we saw a particularly memorable and remarkable sight. A bush was covered with fireflies, all with their bright pinpoints of light flashing on and off synchronously together like a tree of nature's fairy lights!

In the surrounding jungle there was a multitude of spiders. One large, highly conspicuous brightly-striped spider could be seen commanding the centre of a huge web measuring several feet across. Each of the spider's long legs would be stretched out and placed on an outward radiating spoke of the web, which had what I can only describe as a 'spring-like 'zigzag' section built into it. This obviously served to amplify

36

the vibrations of any captive prey. The spider from its central position could by means of its legs, feel the amplified vibrations and so determine the web-site address of its prey!

I'm not sure how a leech is classified in the natural order of things but this was also an unwelcome visitor from the jungle during monsoon. Occasionally I would suffer a visit from a leech without realising it; unknowingly having picked it up as I walked between the college buildings. On a couple of occasions when undressing for bed I found a leech attached high up on my thigh; bloated to giant proportions with the blood it had extracted - yet I hadn't felt a thing! They could be removed with a sprinkling of salt but afterwards the puncture wound would bleed freely because of the anti-coagulant the leech injects to make its bloodsucking easier. My Bhutanese colleagues told me there were several different kinds of leech in the jungles of Bhutan and they are not all confined to the ground. One kind drops on you from the trees above and yet another live in streams and enter the nostrils of cattle as they drink. In the rainy season, when villagers have to travel through the jungle they walk under an umbrella held in one hand to give protection from leeches dropping from above; whilst in the other they carry a stick with a bag of salt tied to the end, with which they dab the leeches rising from the ground. It made me thankful that my personal experience was limited to just one kind!

On rare occasions larger forms of wildlife paid a visit - like one meeting I had in my bathroom at Kharbandi! Having returned from a trip to Thimphu and endured the six-and-a-half hour bus ride without access to a toilet, I was just desperate for one by the time I reached my quarters. My European pedestal type toilet had a low-level cistern situated immediately behind the seat. I had only settled there for a few seconds when I became aware of something moving behind me! Cautiously looking round, I found to my consternation a fairly large bat hanging from the bottom of the cistern; its face and mouth and most significantly its teeth, only about six inches from my bare backside. I stood up as slowly as I dared and attempted to pull up my pants and trousers as unhurriedly as possible; to affect an escape from the six foot by six foot bathroom without disturbing the bat! To my great consternation, even before I had hoisted my trousers, the bat took off and flew round and round me in the close confine of the bathroom! What to do? How could I escape from the bats unwelcome company and get it out of the door - which thankfully was open, without it or me coming to harm?

Remembering that I'd hastily stood my umbrella against the wall outside in my rush to get to the toilet; very slowly and somewhat hampered by my trousers round the ankles, I shuffled crouching toward the door and managed to retrieve my brolly. Cowering behind the open umbrella I reasoned its fabric should reflect back the bat's sonar signals and hopefully persuade it to move away from me. So armed with the umbrella I went on the offensive and manoeuvred the airborne menace toward the door! Much to my relief the strategy worked and the intruder was successfully evicted back to freedom - and we both regained our composure! It was most probably a fruit bat and may not have posed a threat but you can never be too careful; especially in a country where rabies is endemic and carried by bats. The moral of this story is that when you use a toilet in Bhutan always go equipped with an umbrella!

With jungle surrounding the campus, snakes and lizards of

various kinds would also find their way into the college from time to time. One day a huge cobra was discovered coiled in the corner of a classroom; it was so big that the only safe way to remove it was to get a policeman from the nearby police post to shoot it first. Also resident in the jungle round about were very large, scaly, monitor like lizards, two to three feet in length. These were not often seen but on one occasion such a giant lizard was found inside the woodwork shop. The class all stopped work and with much yelling and banging chased the poor terrified creature; until with its tongue spitting rapidly in and out it found its way out of the door and escaped back to the cover and safety of the jungle!

There were a number of Indian nationals on the staff who being Hindu did not have the same aversion to eating meat as did the Buddhist Bhutanese. On one occasion one of them invited staff round to share in a buffet type meal. A dish containing curried chunks of meat was said to be chicken based. Next morning it was disclosed that it was not chicken at all but – yes you've guessed it - the flesh of a giant lizard; whereupon a staff member who had enjoyed eating the dish the night before; stepped outside and vomited at the thought!

Bhutan is almost exclusively Buddhist and to kill most animals is regarded as a sin; however, for some obscure reason the eating of pork and chicken is permitted. Meat was comparatively expensive to buy in the local market (killed and sold by Indian butchers) but any edible animal found in the jungle was 'fair game' for the Indian staff if it could be caught. On one occasion I was invited (strictly as an observer) to join in a night hunt for jungle fowl - a small kind of wild chicken that was quite common and apparently very good to eat, as well as being free game. Along with several of the

Indian members of staff who went armed with catapults, I crept through the jungle in the pitch black of a moonless night. If anything was heard or moved, either in the undergrowth beneath or in the trees above; torch beams were directed like searchlights seeking out their quarry - and the catapults let fly. Very sadly the only thing to be bagged that night was a little owl that was lit up sitting on a branch. Mistaken for a roosting jungle fowl it was dropped in a puff of feathers before it could say 'whooo goes there?'! I have no doubt that it found its way into an Indian cooking pot.

Kharbandi being right on the border with India experienced its share of extreme weather. A few months after my arrival we were caught in the edge of a cyclone centred over Bangladesh and I watched in horror as the galvanised roof of the automobile workshop was completely stripped back like a banana skin and sent flying wildly through the air in bits at high speed. Next morning staff recounted how the previous year it had been the welding shop roof that was destroyed and the year before that, one of the other buildings and so on. It was it seemed a regular occurrence and so of no real note. On another occasion an electric storm, the like of which I had never experienced before, lasted three days and nights with forked lightning and ear-splitting thunder. A lightning bolt hit the electricity line directly outside my living quarters and the sizable power cable instantly vaporised along its whole length and fell gently to earth as ash!

On another occasion suddenly there was a tremendous deafening drumming on the tin roof of my flat and I looked out to see hailstones the size of golf balls falling and rapidly covering the ground like snow. The hail storm was so intense it stripped all the trees and bushes almost bare of leaves. One of the stray dogs that lived around the college campus was running for all it was worth to gain shelter under a parked lorry - no doubt believing it was suffering a particularly heavy onslaught of missiles. The many stray dogs on the loose that roam in Bhutan are discouraged from approaching too close as dogs can carry rabies! When a person gets bitten the only course of treatment to avoid an excruciatingly painful death, is a very unpleasant series of injections in the stomach. Exactly a week later a second hail storm occurred with even bigger hailstones – this time the size of cricket balls - and with spikes on! These smashed almost all of the workshop windows and even punched holes through the asbestos roof of the Principal's living quarters. Having suffered hail storms two Saturdays running, a rumour began to circulate that the next week hailstones the size of footballs would fall; fortunately this prediction never came to pass!

To satisfy the curiosity of my students I wrote to the British Meteorological Office at Bracknell to find out about the formation of hail. They obligingly sent back very interesting information explaining why and how such large hailstones are formed over Bhutan. When water vapour is shunted up and down between a layer of hot air from the plain of India and a strata of cold air from the Tibetan plateaux; water droplets are turned to ice and gradually enlarged layer upon layer as they oscillate up and down; until gravity eventually takes over and brings them down to earth - or something like that! Apparently, the largest hailstone on record in the world, fell in nearby Bangladesh and weighed in at more than a couple of Kilograms!

The unusual climatic conditions over Bhutan also gave rise on occasions to the most dramatic sunsets. As a keen photographer I had taken many pictures of lovely sunsets in Britain, yet on the occasion of the most spectacular sunset I have **ever** seen I didn't have my camera with me! Dawa and I were strolling one evening on the road below the campus where there is a panoramic open vista over the plain of India. As the great orange orb of the setting sun sank below the distant horizon it highlighted the cloud formation overhead in a most amazing and spectacular way. There appeared to be two distinctly separate layers of cloud, one much higher than the other. One layer stretched across the sky in a roughly east - west direction and the lower one at 90* to the first, extended in a north - south direction; so that the combined cloud effect was of an open patchwork or lattice. The setting sun illuminated and coloured each of the two layers quite differently. The overall effect was stunningly beautiful and both Dawa and I stood mesmerised; watching nature weave its transient pattern of light and colour until all too soon with the gathering dusk, the beauty faded and disappeared for ever. Even *if* I had had my camera with me, it could never have captured adequately the quite *extraordinary* majesty, tranquillity and beauty of that particular sunset.

"Give thanks for the harvest of beauty, for that which the hands cannot hold,
The harvest eyes only can gather and only our hearts can enfold."

Chapter 4

TEACHING plus Unexpected Extras

Kharbandi was the only technical college in Bhutan and students having successfully completed five years of primary education in their home district, came there from all over the country to study for a further five years in one of several engineering disciplines. In addition to their specialist technical subjects; they also had to study the English Language, Mathematics, and the national language Dzongkha.

Because no other nation on earth speaks Dzongkha which is the official language of Bhutan; all teaching from the first year of Primary school onwards is conducted in English and virtually all the text books in use are written in English - mostly published in India. This makes it very easy for teachers from English-speaking nations such as Britain, Canada, Ireland, and New Zealand; to teach in Bhutan. Qualified teachers were being recruited through organisations similar to Voluntary Service Overseas from all of these countries and were now being appointed at both primary and secondary level.

The overall literacy rate in Bhutan in 1984 was only reckoned to be eighteen per cent for the population as a whole; because the majority of adults had never had a chance to attend school. Now, encouraged by the government, many parents were realising the advantages and benefits that an education could bring their children and were prepared to make considerable personal sacrifice to afford them the chance to learn to read and write – a chance most of them had never had.

I began teaching within a day or so of arriving at Kharbandi and I will certainly never forget the first time I entered a classroom with some trepidation, to take a lesson. The students all stood *'as one'*, bowed at the waist *'as one'*, greeted me with, 'Good morning La' with one accord and remained standing until told to be seated! Such courtesy was a far cry from what I had been used to in Britain and proved to be more than an initial polite response to impress this teacher from a far off land. Throughout my years at Kharbandi the students without exception were the epitome of politeness. No-one could have wished for more diligent, courteous or enthusiastic students.

It was a pleasant surprise to find that the college had well equipped Mechanical, Electrical, Motor Vehicle, Welding and Carpentry workshops, plus a Drawing Office; all equipped through the United Nations Development Programme. There was a separate administrative and classroom block in which the college library was housed. The library turned out to include some very odd books for a technical college; including one that intrigued me no end, my having just come from Tonbridge in Kent - the *'Root Stock of Fruit Trees Developed at East Malling, Kent'*! What this was doing in a technical college library in Bhutan and how it found its way there, remains a mystery.

Students were meant to be aged sixteen or over before commencing study at Kharbandi but there were no birth certificates in Bhutan and boys seldom knew precisely how old they were. Matters were complicated because being a Tibetan Buddhist country, the belief is that the nine months a

44

child spends in the womb is the first year of life - so you are already a one-year old when new born! Should a child's birthday happen to be near the end of a Bhutanese lunar calendar year; immediately the next year began the child was reckoned as being two years old! Consequently, a boy might be only fourteen by our reckoning and yet in Bhutan legitimately claim to be sixteen! Each year it was obvious that some students barely fourteen had somehow managed to gain admission.

The whole of the education system was still in its infancy and primary schooling was not yet accessible to every child of normal primary school age. Some pupils could be much older than we might expect when they started primary school; which in turn meant some would be approaching twenty by the time they progressed to Kharbandi. The resulting over-all age range of students at Kharbandi College therefore, was from just over fourteen years old; up to possibly twenty-five years old for a few late starters by the time they were nearing the end of their five years of technical training.

When I first arrived I found that much of the teaching was by rote. When students realised that I welcomed rather than discouraged discussion and questions, the lessons were never long enough. Even after the last lesson of the day students would linger to gather every last crumb of learning they could; such was their appreciation of the opportunity given them of furthering their education beyond primary level - a privilege only afforded to a relatively small number in Bhutan at that time.

The normal day for students was a long one; beginning at six thirty in the morning with Buddhist prayers followed by private study in the main college hall - which was staffed on a rota basis. When my turn came around to supervise the early morning study from six thirty until breakfast at eight, it made for a very long week. At the end of each day I had to cook etc. for myself, as well as later I was made responsible for caring for boys in the sick bay; which was the first of my 'Unexpected Extras'.

When on duty in the early morning study period; being English 'born and bred' it was naturally but erroneously thought by students that I would be an expert in the English language - my weakest subject at school. Students plied me with all manner of questions that seemed to me obscure points of grammar; technicalities that I had never heard of, let alone understood! Their questions reflected the method by which English was being taught in Bhutan mainly by Indian nationals and which I imagine dated back to how it was once taught throughout the British Empire; more from a viewpoint of grammatical correctness than to gain a contemporary working knowledge of spoken English. After I'd been teaching at Kharbandi for some months, one of the Indian staff who had received a private education in an Indian mission school told me quite bluntly that I did not speak proper English! He was probably right but I must confess that even when my ear had become attuned to the Indian accent I was still at a loss at times to know what was being said! It seemed yet another example of 'two great nations separated by a common language'.

Before formal lessons commenced at nine, all the students and staff gathered outdoors on the basket ball court for the singing of Bhutan's national anthem. As a foreign national and as a Christian I was excused from singing the anthem, but I had to attend.

In the Thunder Dragon Kingdom
Adorned with sandalwood
The protector who guards the
Teachings of the dual system
He, the precious and glorious ruler,
Causes dominion to spread
While his unchanging person
abides in constancy.
As the doctrine of the Lord Buddha
flourishes,
May the sun of peace and happiness
Shine on the people.

This was of course sung in Dzongkha and with great respect. For a few weeks the decorum of these occasions broke down when the pitch of the singing upset the sensitive hearing of one of the many undomesticated dogs that roamed the campus. Each morning as soon as the singing began, a young puppy with unusually large ears would throw back its head and howl very loudly and mournfully; much to the amusement of the students and staff (and the annoyance of the Bhutanese Acting Principal who had no sense of humour); whereupon the students (and staff) dissolved into fits and giggles of suppressed laughter! When this disruption had been suffered for several weeks the offending puppy mysteriously disappeared, never to be seen or more importantly, heard again!

The more formal classroom subjects of Mathematics, English, Engineering Drawing and Design, Workshop Technology, and Dzongkha, were taught in the mornings; and Workshop practice took place each afternoon until four. After lessons, the end of the day was given over to various sporting activities - through to evening private study until an eagerly awaited supper time. This timetable applied Monday to Friday. On Saturdays there were formal lessons only in the morning and in the afternoon students were organised into work parties to tackle various maintenance tasks around the campus.

Each weekday morning, I would teach Mathematics, and Engineering Drawing and Design, to senior students. In the afternoons I ran a Drawing Office equipped with good professional drafting machines supplied through the UNDP - housed in the same block as the Mechanical Engineering workshop. The college electricity supply came from India and was definitely AC - alternating current; it went off and on all the time! We suffered frequent power cuts which brought the workshop machinery to a standstill. Such cuts invariably occurred in the afternoons when students were engaged in workshop practice and so maximum disruption was caused to the teaching programme. The rest of the staff accepted power cuts as an inevitable everyday fact of life and what's more they afforded a welcome break from teaching - especially when the temperature was soaring!

I found the students a real joy to teach and in Mathematics they were generally very able at solving the usual run of mathematical problems in algebra, geometry, trigonometry, etc.; provided the method for tackling that particular type of problem had been clearly demonstrated. However, most students had absolutely no idea whatever how to solve problems requiring any degree of logical reasoning on their part. It is essential however, that when seeking to solve many practical engineering problems; that by a series of logical deductions and decisions you can arrive at a satisfactory working solution.

It seemed to me, that the method generally used at that time of teaching by rote, didn't encourage students to think problems through logically. Consequently, not long after I began to teach at Kharbandi; at the end of each week I would set my students a logic problem - the type of problem you commonly find in puzzle books; where from a set of clues various deductions can be made that lead to the eventual solution. I was careful to present each problem in a totally Bhutanese context and offered a small weekly prize for the best correct solution; one which clearly and logically demonstrated how the answer had been arrived at. Though the attempts handed in for scrutiny showed that a problem had been grappled with by most of the class (sometimes collectively), only one student out of a class of forty showed any aptitude whatever in the actual application of logic. Some of the solutions received were absolutely hilarious and in many the argument presented was so obtuse that I was the one at a total loss to understand their logic at all!

As soon as my students began to get to know me well enough, they started to ask questions about my family, my country, British customs, my previous college, etc. and how life at home compared to that in Bhutan. A calendar with scenes from around Britain was a focus of great interest and I was quizzed at length about so many details in the pictures that were strange to them. I especially remember trying to describe what the sea was like as they had never seen an ocean. In turn I was able to learn about their families and village life and to glean something of their social and cultural background.

Most of my students came from remote villages. From homes without electricity, without plumbing and without sanitation, let alone any domestic mechanical or electrical aids - the things we take so much for granted in the West! They had never even seen pictures in magazines or books of electrical or mechanical products, nor as children had they played with constructional toys of any kind. There was absolutely nothing in their backgrounds to help them gain even a rudimentary appreciation of the way the simplest mechanical or electrical device worked. Teaching Engineering Drawing presented a particularly interesting challenge; how do you impart in the space of just five years the knowledge and skill to produce and read engineering drawings, to students from the most non-technical background imaginable? Surprisingly, by the end of three years most students were reasonably proficient at producing and reading drawings of quite complex components and assemblies.

The Drawing Office at Kharbandi backed onto the jungle and termites, common throughout the southern region of Bhutan, had eaten out the insides of all of the window frames. They *looked* reasonably sound, as the termites had wisely left intact what was probably a poisonous lead based covering of paint; but below this the frames were mostly eaten through and hollow and you could easily stick your finger into them!

One extremely interesting task I was asked to undertake was to make the very first scale drawings of the wooden framework of a Bhutanese house. Amazingly, the beautiful traditional village houses, the cantilever bridges and even the massive Dzongs, were built without the use of metal fixings of any kind (not even nails) and more surprisingly, without the aid of any drawings. For centuries the knowledge as to how to build them had been passed down only by word of mouth and by example. As young people were now moving away from their village roots, so the old tradition of passing on practical knowhow by an unwritten process of instruction was likely to break down. The time had now come for these skills to be taught more formally so there was a requirement for both formal training to promote construction skills and for working drawings to be produced.

The College had engaged an experienced Bhutanese carpenter to formally teach trainees in the construction of the intricate wooden framework that forms the main structure of a traditional house. At the end of the first house-building course when the wooden framework with its multiplicity of joints and other features was complete, I produced a set of technical drawings showing the various timber components that made up the structure and how they all jointed together. My good friend Dawa was responsible for managing the course and with his help all the different parts of the framework were labelled in Dzongkha along with their English equivalents. It was a fascinating task and one that I thoroughly enjoyed and felt privileged to have committed to paper for the very first time. I would have loved to have had the opportunity to produce similar drawings for the beautiful traditional cantilever bridges, which sadly in time are all too likely to disappear and be replaced with steel cable and concrete bridges.

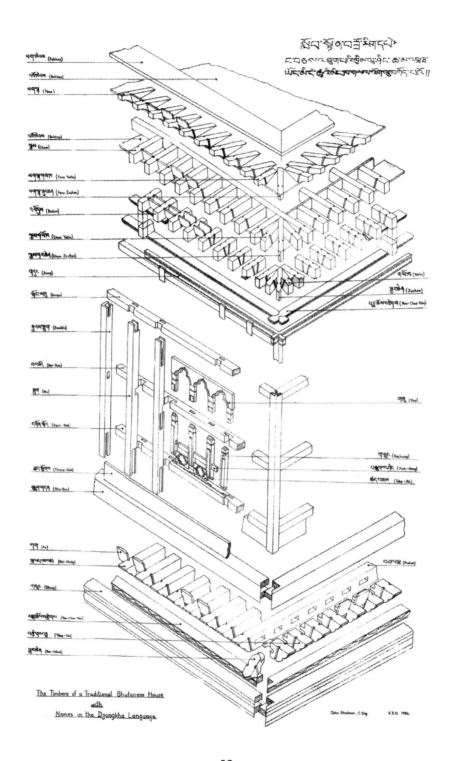

The Timbers of a Traditional Bhutanese House
with
Names in the Dzongkha Language.

The traditional carpenter in Bhutan didn't use a tape measure or square but prior to his starting to build a house made a special right-angled wooden template with various notches cut into its sides. All of the dimensions and proportions required to fashion the complex framework were then taken from this template and when the house is finished the template resides in the altar room – an integral part of every Bhutanese house.

A whole world of difference separated such ancient practices in house building, from the construction of an enormous hydroelectric plant under way about two hours drive up the main road from Kharbandi toward Thimphu, that I was able to visit twice with parties of senior students whilst it was still being built. It was hardly surprising, given the scale and extent of the construction that both the students and the staff who were with me, had some difficulty in comprehending what they were seeing for the first time.

A massive dam across the Wong Chu River was almost complete, and from just above the dam two tunnels had been excavated four kilometres through the mountain to reach a 'Butterfly Control Chamber'. The students had never been into a tunnel before and at first clung to one another for emotional support! When we reached the chamber hewn out from inside the mountain, it was very impressive mining on a huge scale – but more was to follow! From this chamber the water flow into the turbines below would be regulated and two very steeply inclined 'pressure shafts' were being excavated to convey the water at great pressure down some eighty metres into the turbines below.

We were then taken into the 'Turbine Hall' which was truly

enormous and dwarfed the Butterfly Chamber in its cavernous size! It was also hewn out of the inside of the mountain and would house four large turbines that were in various stages of assembly; each of which would generate some eighty megawatts of electricity. We were able to go underneath one turbine under construction; and my students looked awestruck at the massive Pelton Wheel and the huge steel nozzle that would direct and control the powerful jet of water driving the wheel.

An electrical generator was sited immediately above and turned by, each Pelton Wheel; generating the electricity as it rotates, and this electrical power is transmitted via many large cables to a sub-station; simply bristling with high voltage wiring and rows of insulators which must have appeared like something from outer space to my students!

Other than the dam higher up river, the sub-station was the only thing to be seen outside the mountain; apart from the power lines and pylons conveying the power down to India. The whole project was designed and built by Indian engineers and almost all the power generated would go to India. It was possible that some of my students could be posted to this hydroelectric plant at some time in the future, and it was good to be able to help them understand how it operated to convert the potential energy of the water stored at the dam, into electrical energy. The great thing for the environment is that not only is most of the generating plant hidden inside the mountain but also that the diverted water from the Wong Chu River once it has passed through the turbines, is all fed back into the river once more. This great leap forward in technology would face my students and Bhutan in the near future and it is difficult to appreciate the extent of the adjustment in thinking required.

The only blueprint copying machine for duplicating large working drawings - probably in the whole of Bhutan at that time, was in 'my' Drawing Office. As well as it being used to reproduce drawings for mechanical workshop exercises; periodically I would be asked to copy drawings for various UN development personnel - so it was a rather vital and valued facility and was another 'Unexpected Extra' responsibility for me. On returning to Kharbandi after my first summer break, I was dismayed to discover that inexplicably the blueprint machine was no longer working. When the usual electrical checks failed to pinpoint any problem I removed its top outer casing to investigate further; to discover that the internal wiring together with much of the canvas conveyor belt that formed an important part of its workings, was chewed into small pieces! Suddenly a large rat jumped from inside the machine and made a rapid escape under the Drawing Office door! Shortly after this, I uncovered a whole nest of young rats closeted in the shredded remains of the inside of our precious blueprint machine! Two students quickly disposed of the rat-brats and I was left to patch the machine back together as best I could; as obtaining spares for any equipment in Bhutan was either impossible or likely to take many months. Such were the joys of working close to nature!

At the end of formal lessons each weekday, members of staff were encouraged to join the students in a programme of sporting activity. The most popular sport in Bhutan is archery and has a huge following among the male population. It might be equated with golf in Britain as the most social sport in which to participate. However, an archery match normally lasts at least a day, so at Kharbandi archery was reserved for weekends and national holidays. Provided it was dry and cool enough, football was by far the most popular sport and there were two football pitches on campus. Cricket was played when the weather was hot and this was another firm favourite - especially with the Indian staff. As I was a keen badminton player and had coached students at home, I created four outdoor badminton courts and encouraged an interest in this sport. Badminton has long been popular in India where all the necessary equipment was easily sourced.

Archery is played by the men of Bhutan at every level from inter-village matches to national tournaments, and they are all keenly contested. There is a target at both ends of the archery pitch which is about 130 metres long; each target consisting of a board about three feet high by a foot wide with a bull's-eye marked near the top and the aim is to hit the target or get closer to it than your opponents closest arrow. Bows are traditionally made from bamboo but during my time at Kharbandi western style composite bows were beginning to appear and to change the nature of the game. An archery match lasts all day and sometimes more than one day and every team member stops work to play in it – even the staff of a hospital! The craziest part of Bhutanese archery is that as you are in the act of firing the opposing team dances, singing and shouting, in front of the target to put you off your aim! Needless to say some accidents occur!

Just three days after I arrived at Kharbandi an accident happened on the football pitch that was to have a considerable impact on my life. Bhutan proudly boasted a national youth soccer team and they had stopped off for a warm-up match against our college eleven on their way to participate in an international all Asia Tournament in New Delhi. During the keenly contested game there was a collision between their centre forward and the Kharbandi goalkeeper. Even from the touch line I heard the loud crack of a breaking bone and unfortunately their forward had fractured both main bones in his lower leg. It was then that I discovered to my great consternation, that I was the only person on hand with knowledge of first aid. So it fell to me to apply an improvised splint and organise a makeshift stretcher to convey the distressed lad for treatment to the cottage hospital in Phuentsholing.

This unfortunate accident made it obvious that some training in first aid was badly needed at Kharbandi. I had completed a fairly comprehensive First Aid course at my college just before leaving for Bhutan hoping it might prove useful - but little did I guess what it would lead to! Subsequently, once a week after formal lessons, I gave first aid training to all students in their final year. This was another 'Unexpected Extra' but one that I believed was extremely worthwhile and a most rewarding extension to my teaching duties. What we lacked in resources (the quality of the only available bandages from India was abysmal - so loosely woven there was more space than bandage), the students more than made up for in enthusiasm. They were just so eager to learn all they could and thoroughly enjoyed either role playing as the patient or acting as the first aider. We covered the procedure and treatment for every different injury in the First Aid Manual (also included in my luggage). Hopefully, when they would come to leave the college and be posted by Government to work in technical support roles all over the country; their first aid training would not be forgotten and might some day prove useful.

At the end of the first course when I had covered all the usual procedures, we came to the last topic in my first aid manual - emergency child birth! Never having had to deliver a baby myself I imagined my students might well know more about this subject than I did, so I planned to give the topic only scant coverage. However, I was proved wrong. They told me that during delivery Bhutanese males are usually kept well away until it is all over. Consequently, my all male class was very eager to learn what they could about child birth. On the day I dealt, as best I could, with *'emergency child birth'* - only in theory you understand; I had 100 per cent attendance and 110 per cent attention!

Following this first added extra to the course I was further requested to present a lesson dealing with more general sex education issues! This was certainly _not_ covered in my **'Engineers Handbook'** and would call for considerable diplomacy in how it should be handled. Working on the principle that to be forewarned is to be forearmed, I invited written questions to be handed in to the Head Boy beforehand. This gave me a chance to consider my response and decide what might be the most appropriate information and advice to give. Again, the students were so appreciative of my efforts (given with tongue in cheek) and this final session proved highly illuminating to say the least, as they also shared with me some of the practices and attitudes to sex in their culture!

It was then suggested that the same first aid course be given for staff (without the extras). Though this course was made compulsory and conducted outside their normal teaching hours, the staff entered into the spirit of the thing with great enthusiasm and proved far harder to control than the students!

I was then requested to operate a 'sick bay' to check out boys who claimed to be ill, and if appropriate to provide basic care to those cases which proved to be genuine. My medical knowledge is strictly limited and though I was capable of taking a temperature and treating minor scrapes and injuries, as well as treating simple ailments like boils - a common affliction; I was careful to refer anything that might be serious to a doctor in Phuentsholing. I was assisted in the sick bay by two willing senior students, Yeshi and Sonam, eager to assist in whatever way they could and who often got to the root of a problem quicker and easier than I did.

One boy came to the sick bay complaining of a problem with his eyes. His pupils were extremely dilated and the bright sunlight was causing him a lot of pain. I had no idea what might have caused such a condition but with Yeshi's help we got to the root of his problem. The boy had suffered some eye irritation and so he'd used the *'eye ointment'* prescribed by a doctor for **another** student months earlier to treat an eye after it had been hit by a football. This misuse of medication was quite common, as there was no understanding of modern drugs and their usage whatsoever.

During the time I taught at Kharbandi I had to carry out most of the procedures in the first aid manual: dressing lacerations and treating burns, scalds, breaks and abrasions, etc., in fact, doing most things apart from delivering a baby! The First Aid Manual was always to hand as was the invaluable book **'Where there is no Doctor'**.

On one occasion I had to deviate from all the advice given in first aid when a student came to me with a fly trapped inside his ear. The recommended method for removal of a foreign object from the ear is to flood it with water or oil, so expelling the foreign body - but the lad had an unusually small access to the inner part of his ear and the fly would not be budged. I could hear it buzzing loudly and it must have been like having a jack hammer in your head. As a last resort and to relieve the obvious distress he was in, I had to do what the manual said should never be done; that is insert a pair of tweezers into the ear, knowing full well what damage I could cause if the lad moved during the procedure. My helper Yeshi held the lad's head firmly against a wall so that he could not move forwards or backwards, whilst I carried out the extraction with the greatest of care, so as not to damage his ear drum. Very gradually, with millimetre by millimetre precision I advanced then withdrew the tweezers, until much to his delight and my relief the fly came out at last, gripped between the prongs.

In the south of Bhutan malaria is widespread and to avoid catching it, it was necessary for me to take an anti-malarial drug every day and sleep under a mosquito net. Many students did not have a net and as they slept in dormitories, malaria could be all too readily transmitted from one boy to another by mosquito bite. Eventually I managed to get a weekly supply of quinine tablets to give some protection to the students. Once a week during the early morning study period, the foul-tasting pill had to be personally administered to each of the three hundred plus boys gathered in the hall to make quite sure that they swallowed it! Followed by a helper equipped with a bucket of water and a cup, we could do the rounds of all 300+ boys in about ten minutes! If that sounds unhygienic, all Bhutanese have a very neat skill of drinking from a cup or bottle without it touching their lips!

Unfortunately, not all the problems encountered at Kharbandi were overcome as simply. The end-of-year examinations was held each December and after only three months in post I found myself responsible for setting the final paper in Engineering Drawing and Design. Having set and marked many examination papers during my previous twenty years of teaching, I was familiar with the safeguards followed to ensure papers are set and marked properly and fairly. I also realised that my first exam paper at Kharbandi, and the way I set and marked it would be closely watched. I took extra care to ensure the questions reflected the syllabus and the level of work taught; that the marking scheme was properly constructed; that marking was thorough and that the results reflected the achievement of each candidate in relation to the others.

When all the marking was finished for all the various papers sat a special staff meeting was called to 'review' the exam results. I was shocked when during the meeting, staff were directed to alter certain marks. They were to be 'adjusted' in a most unprofessional and illogical manner; not to maintain any particular level of pass rate but to ensure that certain students gained passes in subjects that they had manifestly failed! This 'upgrading' was being done across all subjects including mine, with the exception of Dzongkha. To be confronted with such flagrant rigging of results presented me with my first major professional dilemma at Kharbandi.
Never had I come across corruption or abuse of the examination system whilst teaching in Britain and it was clearly unethical to allow such rigging of results to go unchallenged. Being the only non-Asian on the staff and the

only one with experience of exam practice elsewhere; it left me no choice but to object to such 'adjustment' of marks and express my disquiet. I was careful at the same time to make constructive counter proposals on how to put the grading of candidates on a proper statistical and ethical footing. There ensued a prolonged, embarrassing and difficult exchange between me and the then Bhutanese Acting Principal, who it transpired, was the instigator of the whole thing. The dispute dragged on between us over several weeks; and when all constructive suggestion on my part as to how to ensure the system was fair was very rudely dismissed out of hand; I came very close to resigning and returning to Britain.

The majority of staff were honest and conscientious and had no wish to meddle with exam results. They were being overruled by the Acting Principal who was bending the rules to serve his own ends. In retrospect I'm glad I didn't resign, as gradually over the remainder of my time at Kharbandi I witnessed significant strides forward to ensure future examinations were conducted on a sound and proper footing. This was especially so when in the spring of 1986 after sixteen months, my isolation as the only non-Asian staff member came to an end and support arrived in the form of three more British VSO's and a new Principal appointed by the British Council.

As the VSO programme in Bhutan expanded and the number of volunteers increased, so it became necessary for a VSO Field Office to be opened in Thimphu. A Field Director, Mark Goldring, was appointed and proved to be both capable and helpful and was able to make life considerably easier for me; in practical ways such as approving the purchase of a small refrigerator; as well as in discussions behind the scenes to bring about an improved working relationship between the Bhutanese Acting Principal and myself, which had not been over cordial. It was so good to have someone at hand to discuss your problems and difficulties with and to make you feel less out on a limb and a part of the larger scheme of things. In time, more volunteers arrived through the VSO programme including other teachers; filling posts across Bhutan in primary and secondary schools - some in the most remote locations imaginable. As travel was so difficult and volunteers were scattered all over the country, we would usually only meet up by chance if we happened to be visiting Thimphu at the same time.

It was a new experience for me to be living as well as working on a college campus. Most Bhutanese had never met anyone from further away than India and my every action was scrutinised with interest. Being the only non-Asian for the first sixteen months I was an object of curiosity and felt at times rather like a goldfish in a bowl. To preserve my sanity, every now and then I needed to get away from the confines of the college. In the first few weeks during any free time I explored the immediate area as far as possible but walking in jungle was a new experience and I was fairly cautious.

There were no expatriates within many miles of Kharbandi and to meet up with other Westerners I had to take a six-and-a-half hour minibus ride to the capital Thimphu, where the few other foreign workers in Bhutan were mostly based. Quite apart from the expense, my duties only made this possible every six weeks or so. On one of my first journeys on the public mini-bus it pulled into the side of the narrow road at one point to allow a lorry to pass. I casually looked out of the window and found myself looking directly into the eyes of the largest owl I have ever seen about six feet away from me! It was I believe a Forest Eagle Owl and 'weighs' in at over two feet tall! To travel up to Thimphu on a Friday and return on a Monday affording me two days to socialise in the capital over a weekend, took a couple of days of special leave for each trip. Never-the-less, such occasional visits to Thimphu were extremely important in relieving the isolation; in enabling me to meet up with other westerners; as well as to enjoy a short break from the college campus and escape the close scrutiny and demands of students.

The capital city Thimphu in those days was not much different to any of the other centres of population in Bhutan except for being somewhat larger. It would be a great stretch of the imagination to describe Thimphu as a metropolis or as humming with life! Surprisingly and totally out of character it boasted a Swiss bakery and coffee shop. This was run by an enterprising Swiss man who had arrived in Bhutan in the early 1960's soon after its borders were first opened. Being the only bakery in Thimphu and a Swiss bakery at that, it was a great draw for the small expatriate community and a favourite meeting place for any based in or visiting Thimphu. Good coffee, crusty bread, fancy cakes, beautiful omelettes and other such goodies were to be had - at a price - at the Swiss bakery! A visit here was a special treat to be savoured and on my return to Kharbandi I would take a decent loaf back with me, to prolong the pleasure.

On one of my visits to Thimphu I met a recently-arrived teacher for the first time. Over a cup of coffee, we casually swapped notes on our respective situations and then got around to discussing our teaching experience before joining VSO.

She asked me, "Where were you teaching before coming out to Bhutan?"

"In Tonbridge, Kent", I replied.

"O really" she said, "I also taught in Kent, in Bromley - and I lived in Catford."

"My daughter lives in Catford - in Ewhurst Road" I replied.

"Well I never, I also lived in Ewhurst Road, number 33!" She exclaimed.

I was absolutely amazed; as my daughter was now living in the very same flat and had done, it seems, from the time it was vacated by this young teacher! Statistically the chance of such a thing occurring must be billions to one!

After sixteen months my isolation was ended when three more VSO's were appointed to work at Kharbandi. Steve Payne from Bournemouth was a motor vehicle mechanic with particular knowledge of heavy diesel vehicles - gained during his service in the army; Michael Reed from Hastings was a machinist with excellent knowledge and skill in the use of machine tools. Then there was Andy a plumber, who having served his time in a shipyard in Birkenhead was at last able to bring order out of the chaos of the college water supply! A fourth VSO, Dave from Yorkshire when he first arrived was going to change the world single-handed but after only three weeks decided he was not cut out for the job after all and returned home!

After Dennis Lee the new Principal had been in post for a few months, the Acting Principal was sent to Britain for teacher training – not a moment too soon. I often wondered whether it made any difference to the way he managed things when

65

he returned! There were fundamental problems to be addressed at Kharbandi and the arrival of these new members of staff was an important mile stone. Key members of the Bhutanese staff were also then sent to Britain for teacher training whilst the VSO's provided cover for courses to continue in their absence. Standards began to improve as fundamental management changes were made and as the outside experience and practical expertise of these VSO's was brought to bear. More efficient use was made of college resources; teaching standards were raised; and a start was made on the introduction of new courses such as electronics that would enable Bhutan to meet its future needs with the increasing exposure to the technological age that would accompany development.

On a personal level, though I'd made good friends and formed a relationship with several staff families over the previous sixteen months, it was now really good to have compatriots that I could also socialise with and talk over shared problems. The sense of isolation I'd felt keenly sometimes during those early months came to an end. Now there were others who saw situations from my perspective and shared some of my frustrations over things like the water supply or lack of it and the mail that went astray etc.! More importantly, we could support one another in working toward a shared objective to improve standards and establish good practice throughout the college.

The students at Kharbandi came from across the whole country and from all three main ethnic groups found in Bhutan. Most of the population in the North West of Bhutan is predominantly 'Bhutia' - people descended from Tibetans who came into Bhutan many centuries ago. Those in the east are 'Sherdukpen' and are believed to be the descendants of the people who originally populated this region of the Eastern Himalaya. Both of these ethnic groups are Mongoloid in origin and their facial features, temperament and culture are very similar. The third ethnic group is of Nepali origin and mainly lived in the south of the country. These were descended from people who colonised the south of Bhutan just a hundred years or so ago and are Aryan in origin, originally from the Indian plains. Their facial appearance, temperament, religion and culture are distinctly different to those of the other two groups. Though all were Bhutanese citizens, it soon became clear that there were significant differences between these three main groups.

From 1984 – 87 throughout my first three years, Bhutan was truly the 'Land of the Peaceful Dragon'. There was no ethnic strife despite the cultural and ethnic differences. All were 'Bhutanese' having been born and brought up in Bhutan and having attended school in Bhutan. They owned allegiance to the King of Bhutan and were proud to be counted as one of His subjects. Sadly, this was all about to change.

Until 1987 Bhutan was a very peaceful country and the Government actively encouraged 'intermarriage' between individuals from the different ethnic groups, by offering a cash incentive to any entering into a 'mixed marriage'. On the surface there was little indication of the ethnic strife that was to come and only in looking back, can I see with hindsight that the seeds of discontent and future conflict were already taking root.

The Royal Government brought in a stipulation that to progress from one year of studies to the next through the education system, students **had** to pass an examination in the national language Dzongkha at the end of each academic year. Failure to pass in future, would mean an automatic end to ones continuing education. This seems reasonable on the face of it, until one realises that Dzongkha is the native language only of the Bhutia people and is totally different in every way to Nepali - the language generally spoken throughout the south of Bhutan and at that time probably the most commonly used language in use in Bhutan.

The national official language of Dzongkha being a tonal language is very difficult to learn to speak and even more difficult to write, yet all internal official communications are in Dzongkha. The new edict put those of Nepali descent - for whom of course Nepali was their native tongue; at a distinct disadvantage within the country's education system and at the same time gave to those who were Bhutia in origin, a distinct advantage over the students from either of the other two ethnic groups. Before I left Kharbandi in 1987 I was becoming aware of a murmur of discontent among some of my students as a result of this ruling but there was no indication of the ethnic strife and suffering that would erupt throughout the south of Bhutan in the very near future.

Chapter 5

Exploring the Dragon Kingdom

During the first sixteen months in Bhutan my trips to Thimphu, though short, helped me a tremendous amount to cope with the trials of working in such an isolated and demanding situation; as well as in relieving the loneliness I felt at times in being cut off from friends and family back home. My occasional visits north also gave me the opportunity on occasions to day-trek in the surrounding mountains and these excursions were particularly memorable. I was a keen walker and had trekked several of the long distance footpaths in Britain including the 'Pennine Way;' and had 'hill-walked' in the mountains of Scotland, Wales, and the Lake District. So I was eager to explore Bhutan on foot as much as possible.

In 1984 there were almost no restrictions as to where you could walk or the places you could visit in Bhutan. The only limitation then in force applied to travel in the sensitive area bordering Chinese occupied Tibet in the very far north. However, though there was complete freedom of movement, there were no maps - not even road maps, let alone maps for trekking. However, ancient mule trails existed connecting towns, villages and monasteries and were still in use and easy to follow.

On one of my very first walks on just such a trail over a pass between Paro and the Gidakom valley, I was suddenly confronted by a lynx - one of the smaller of the 'big' cats. It appeared silently out of the forest about twenty yards in front of me and just stared, as surprised to see me as I was to see it.

After only a few tantalising seconds during which its distinctive tufted ears clearly identified what species of wildcat it was, and without posing any kind of threat; it melted away into the forest again as silently as it had appeared. Bhutan is home to a number of dangerous wild animals including tiger, leopard, wild boar and black bear. When my Bhutanese colleagues at Kharbandi learned that I was walking through forest unarmed they were horrified and promptly presented me with a Nepali style *'Kukre'* or hunting knife, made from the steel of an old lorry spring, that I could use to defend myself in future should the need arise.

Quite apart from the possible threat posed by wild animals, it was also necessary to appreciate that should you get into difficulty, Bhutan did not have any form of mountain rescue service. This was brought home to me in a very telling way on a walk made whilst staying with friends in Thimphu during my first Christmas in Bhutan. Back in 1984 the number of expatriates in Bhutan was very small indeed and mostly employed in the Health Department. Much to my surprise, I discovered that the sister-in-law of someone I had known for many years was working in a senior nursing post at Thimphu General Hospital. She shared a small flat with another nurse but kindly arranged for me during visits to Thimphu to stay with Ray, an English paediatrician who had a guest bedroom. I was delighted to accept their invitation to stay with these new-found friends for my first Christmas in Bhutan, rather than spend it 'alone' at Kharbandi. My hosts were on duty in the hospital for most of the 26th December; so left to my own devices I decided to take the opportunity to do a day-trek, planning to return before dark in time for the special Boxing Day meal.

From Thimphu, I could see what looked to be a monastery high above the valley and I decided to climb up to it on a ridge path that clearly led up the steep open mountainside from the valley floor. I set off after an early breakfast before 8.00 a.m. on a perfectly clear morning to begin my climb. After about an hour's steady ascent, it became obvious that the building was far higher and more distant than it had looked and I finally reached it at around eleven in the morning after another two hours climbing. It turned out not to be a monastery after all but some kind of giant metal reflector, probably to do with the telephone link with India at that time. As I'd reached this initial goal well before midday, the very top of the mountain looked to be attainable in plenty of time to allow me to get safely back down before dark. I anticipated that on such a perfectly clear day the mountaintop would provide a vantage point affording a wonderful view of the Himalayan peaks to the northeast. I was not too worried about the time it might still take to get to the top, knowing that my descent should be very much quicker than the climb up. After a total of six hours I finally reached the top at around two in the afternoon.

The view was every bit as rewarding as I'd hoped, with the great chain of mountain peaks, among the highest in the world, clear in every detail, stretched out before me. Though there was snow on the ground, it was comfortably warm in the winter sunshine and there was no wind. I didn't linger on the top for long as in December the days are short and I was eager to make it back to Thimphu well before dark. I stayed just long enough to snack on some chocolate before starting out on my way down.

On the ascent I had seen a well - trodden alternative path

71

following an adjacent ridge, and had made up my mind that if possible I would take this route, rather than return on the same path. Having found what looked to be the top of this alternative route, I began to make my way down. Imagine my dismay when after descending about a thousand feet mostly through forest, the track suddenly petered out to nothing! It came to a dead end! A full stop! There was not a trace of a path leading further down and I was faced with a real dilemma. Should I retrace my steps climbing the thousand feet or more back to the top and then descend on my original route; or, should I cut laterally across the mountain in the general direction which I knew very well must eventually intersect the downward path I was seeking? After a strenuous day of walking I was beginning to tire and the thought of climbing back up a thousand feet made up my mind for me. I would cut through the forest across the mountainside keeping to roughly the same altitude until I happened upon the desired alternative path that I sought. This proved to be a decision that might well have cost me my life.

Once I began to steer my way through the forest there was no going back, as in the absence of a path I could very easily lose my sense of direction altogether and end up completely lost. After a comparatively short distance I reached a ravine slicing down the mountainside and lying directly across my chosen route. I had little option other than to climb down the fifty feet or so of rock face to the bottom and then up out again on the other side. The gully at the bottom of the ravine was filled with a mass of thick almost impenetrable bamboo, which I only managed to get through by crawling on my hands and knees along a tunnel, obviously frequented by a wild animal of some kind. By the time I had climbed up out of the ravine on the far side my body was soaked in perspiration; my heart

72

pounded at a rapid rate from the effort involved; and my reserves of energy were seriously depleted - bearing in mind that I was at an altitude of about 11000 feet (3350m). On reaching the top I had to lie down and let my heart rate and breathing recover somewhat, before I could continue on in the general direction I knew the sought-for path to be.

Once my heartbeat normalised I pressed on again through the forest. I had only gone a further few hundred metres when to my utter dismay I came to a second ravine, presenting a similar major obstacle to progress. My heart sank but there was now no option other than to press on, as the afternoon was well advanced and I was seriously tired. I climbed down into this second ravine and again managed to negotiate a way through thick bamboo at the bottom as well as over a frozen stream. Summoning all my reserve I eventually managed to climb out of it on the far side. Now desperately tired, I lay for a long time gasping for air and wondering what my chances of survival would be should I be marooned up here for the night? Darkness was now falling, the temperature was plummeting and I was very aware that my underclothes, soaked in perspiration, were beginning to freeze next to my skin. There was no shelter up here from the intense night time cold, I had no means of lighting a fire, no torch, no food and no sleeping bag. All I wanted to do was to lie down and sleep but I knew that that could prove fatal, as at this altitude and at such low temperatures I would very likely suffer from exposure and hypothermia. I prayed for guidance and strength before making one last effort in the fast failing light to find the path I knew existed; before, in the event of failure to do so, I would make myself as comfortable as possible and sit out the hours of darkness.

The words of King David in the Book of Psalms came into

mind: 'I lift up my eyes to the hills, where does my help come from?' 'My help comes from the Lord who made heaven and earth.' Looking up I glimpsed what looked to be the tops of a line of prayer flags and I headed in their direction. After just a further thirty paces or so through the forest, I emerged from the trees and with enormous relief and thankfulness found my self on the sought-for path running down an open ridge. It was now quite dark and far below I could see the distant lights of Thimphu but I knew now that provided I descended with care and kept to the path, I should reach Thimphu safely.

When at last I arrived at my friends' house several hours late for their special meal, they were greatly relieved to see me back safe and sound. I was so exhausted it was a major effort to keep my eyes from closing as I ate the meal they had kindly kept for me. I'm afraid that meal is just a blur in the memory but I do remember drinking glass after glass of water as a result of being so dehydrated from my mountain ordeal. Never again would I contemplate attempting a trek in Bhutan without someone knowing what route I intended to take and making sure that I carried at least the bare essentials for survival should I again experience unforeseen difficulties.

In a comparatively small country like Bhutan news soon travels around the expatriate community of a newcomer joining their number. Not many weeks after I'd started teaching at Kharbandi there was a knock on the classroom door and a Western couple was shown in to meet me. Doctor Gottfried Riedel and his wife Helle were in charge of the work at Gidakom Hospital, from which the leprosy work throughout western Bhutan was coordinated and which housed the most seriously disabled patients needing long-term hospital care. Gidakom was also a teaching hospital, running courses for Bhutanese doctors, nurses and physiotherapists on the diagnosis and treatment of leprosy. They were among the first Leprosy Mission personnel to enter Bhutan at the invitation of the then Prime Minister during the early 1960's, when leprosy was a considerable health problem. The leprosy programme had prospered, until now in 1984 there were leprosy hospitals across Bhutan and a rigorous system in place for annually surveying the whole population to identify new cases. A system of inspection that would eventually bring leprosy under control.

Dr Riedel had heard on the grape-vine that I was working at Kharbandi, and had called to see if we could help in manufacturing in the College workshops, specialised items that were required. For several years at home I had run a group of volunteers engaged in the design and manufacture of all manner of aids for individuals with disabilities. This request for Kharbandi to be involved in practical projects for the leprosy hospital therefore touched a resonant chord. So over the ensuing months students and staff helped in the manufacture and repair of several items for Gidakom hospital. I was then invited to visit Gidakom, situated in a valley between Paro and Thimphu, and from time to time I would enjoy the Riedel's hospitality as well as lend a hand with various practical tasks around the hospital over a weekend or sometimes longer. Working at Gidakom hospital stretched my inventiveness and practical skill, and the range of tasks varied widely. They included drawing up plans for new building, advising on general maintenance work, making new and reconditioning broken equipment, mapping the hospital land to register it for Government records – and turning an old autoclave sterilising unit into a pressure vessel to apply a tourniquet at a given pressure during a surgical operation!

When this tourniquet device was ready for its initial trial, I was 'scrubbed up' and dressed in surgical cap and gown to work it throughout an operation, to be performed in the rather basic operating theatre at Gidakom. A patient now cured of her leprosy was to have the use of a thumb restored by the re-routing of a tendon - a surgical procedure carried out by Dr Riedel. Everything went to plan and after a successful operation and subsequent physiotherapy it was so rewarding to see this lady able to use her thumb again and to grip things. Even though as a direct consequence of leprosy the fingers of her hand had been largely lost - damaged beyond repair by infection; she had now been given back limited but invaluable use of the hand as a result of this surgery.

On one extended visit to Gidakom Hospital I was able to take a trek following an ancient mule trail from the head of Gidakom valley that crosses over a pass to Thimphu on the far side. It was wintertime when conditions are good with firm going underfoot and the sun shining all day out of a brilliant deep blue cloudless sky. I was surprised at first that at such altitudes with the ground frozen solid; when the sun shone it could be so warm you had to strip to just a shirt above the waist.

Because my usual base at Kharbandi was not much above sea level, nearing the top of the pass at about 10500 feet (3200 m), even though I was reasonably fit the rarefied atmosphere made me gasp for breath. My pulse raced so much, I had to stop more and more often as I approached the top to reduce the pounding of my heart and subdue the heaving in my chest. The route was easy enough to follow along a stone-paved mule trail dating from antiquity. I could only imagine the enormous amount of labour involved in the carrying, dressing and laying of these huge stone slabs at this altitude in constructing such a paving.

At the top of the pass I saw my first herd of yak grazing in an alpine type meadow, on patches of grass where the snow had melted. I am told that these interesting animals are so completely adapted to living their lives entirely at altitude, that if they are brought down to less than 8000 feet (2500m) for more than a few days they become sick and will die unless returned again immediately to a higher level. In Bhutan the herds of yak with their minders live most of their lives on the very high altitude pasture of the Himalaya and usually only descend to lower levels during the worst months of winter when the depth of snow prevents them from grazing higher up.

From the top of the pass I laboured my way still higher toward the monastery of Phajoding, which I could see on the mountainside to the north of the pass. I had been told a log cabin existed up here somewhere just beyond the monastery, where I planned to spend the night. Fortunately, I reached the cabin well before dark when with the coming of nightfall the temperature would plummet! I found the cabin locked so it was fortunate I'd been told how to gain access through a rear window!

There were a few dry logs to burn in the makeshift wood stove or 'bukhari' that occupied the centre of one large circular room and this was the only concession to comfort; as there was no water, no lighting, and no toilet facilities! What could you expect at 11500 feet (3500m) up in the mountains in the middle of nowhere? However, what the accommodation lacked in amenities it more than made up for in location and outlook. Large glass windows gave a magnificent panoramic view out over the distant mountain tops and the valleys between. I watched spellbound as the afterglow from the sun faded in the southwest to reveal a fantastic vista of night sky full of brilliantly bright shining stars. The downside of the large single glazed windows was that they gave little resistance to the penetration of the extreme cold, against which the small primitive wood stove in the middle of this sizable room afforded little protection. Lying on the floor I gave thanks for my four season's duck down sleeping bag which had been of no use whatever to me thus far at Kharbandi but here it certainly came into its own! This was the highest bivouac at which I had ever spent a night. I lay down but not to sleep as my heart thumped all night long - a result of altitude - preventing any possibility of even briefly nodding off.

I slid out of my sleeping bag well before the break of dawn, somewhat stiff from lying on the hard wooden floor. After packing my rucksack, I climbed a path the remaining few hundred feet to a ridge overlooking the Thimphu valley thousands of feet below. It was perfectly still without even the hint of a breeze. The silence was absolute. The valley below was completely filled between its encompassing mountains with a blanket of gently undulating white cloud like wall-to-wall cotton wool. I sat there in the perfect stillness, mesmerised by the incredibly beautiful vista open before me. A lovely clear day dawned, with the sky to the east gradually colouring to a bright orange as the sun came closer to rising above the mountain peaks in the far distance. After breakfasting on a bar of chocolate it was with considerable reluctance that I made the move to slowly make my way down the trail that would lead me to Thimphu and back to reality.

The track descended through a natural forest of large pine trees for most of the way. One of the dangers in such an area is the Himalayan Black Bear - common throughout this northern region of Bhutan. If you happen to come face-to-face with one, it will usually attack you on sight and horrific injuries from encounters with these powerful creatures are not uncommon. To avoid such a calamity the Bhutanese hang bells on their leading mules and yak, as well as shouting loudly to one another as they make their way through the forest. Bears will avoid human contact provided they hear you coming. Whenever I might possibly meet with a bear and as there was no-one else within earshot to be troubled by it, I sang at the top of my lungs. Having been blessed with a lusty voice I never once met a bear in my travels!

The steep descent was a much quicker process than the climb up and I soon reached the outskirts of Thimphu. Where the track emerged from the forest on the edge of the town, there was a large penned area containing a single specimen of Bhutan's unique national animal - the Takin. The Takin is a horse-like creature with a humped nose that normally lives up on the very highest pastures above 12000 feet (3700m). I never saw another specimen of this rather special and peculiar high altitude mammal.

Whenever I went to stay at Gidakom, if possible I would purchase a large joint of fresh pork from the Phuentsholing market to take with me as a gift for hospitality; as meat was a rare luxury in Bhutan anywhere other than near the Indian border. On one winter visit it was already dark when the public mini bus from Phuentsholing dropped me off on the main road at its nearest point to Gidakom. I still had several kilometres to walk up the valley in the dark, to reach the hospital. I was carrying a full rucksack on my back as well as a large leg of pork in a cloth shoulder bag, so to lighten the load I hid my rucksack in a ditch and walked on carrying just the bag of meat. I was then able to hitch a ride back down the track to retrieve my rucksack. We had hardly driven more than a few hundred metres when a leopard with a cub in tow crossed in front of the vehicle! I couldn't help thinking about what might have happened had I reached that spot on foot carrying the fresh pork, at the same time as the female leopard and her cub!

When in 1985, Kharbandi closed for its summer break; I went to spend my vacation at Gidakom where the climate is much more pleasant and far less humid than at Kharbandi. One evening I was walking along a path above the hospital, following a channel that conveys water to a small hydroelectric plant that was first built to serve Thimphu. Hearing a commotion, I turned and saw a stag being swept rapidly along in the water course, desperately trying to climb out! The channel ran into a concrete holding reservoir and the flow through this reservoir was controlled by a sluice gate operated by an Indian labourer who lived on site in a wood cabin. I ran down the path and tried to enlist his help in rescuing the poor creature from the water but unfortunately for the deer there was a breakdown in communications and before I could stop him, the man picked up a boulder and hit the animal a fatal blow on the back of the head. Though it was very sad for the deer, I made the best of a bad job by staking my claim to its hind-quarters. We enjoyed the rare luxury of fresh meat and lived like lords off venison for a week, until the very last scraps were used up in a venison cottage pie!

My visits to Gidakom to stay with the Riedel's also stretched me in another way, as they were both keen 'Scrabble' players. We usually passed a pleasant but for me frustrating evening playing 'Scrabble'. They were both native German speakers for whom English was only their second language but, much to my frustration and chagrin, though we played Scrabble in English they always, yes *always* beat me! My friendship with the Riedel's was to span many years and my initial personal involvement with the work at Gidakom Hospital, would lead eventually to my returning to Bhutan to officially work for The Leprosy Mission International.

Chapter 6

A Welcome Christmas Visitor

I'd been at Kharbandi for more than a year when I was thrilled to learn that my daughter was planning to visit and spend Christmas of 1985 with me. During a comparatively short three-week stay we had more than our share of adventure together and even her journey to Bhutan was hardly an auspicious start to the visit.

She'd not been outside of the UK before so, to ensure she actually reached Bhutan, I travelled to Delhi to meet her. It was just as well I did. The day she was due to arrive, thick fog caused her flight to be diverted to Bombay! She finally reached Delhi 26 hours late - quite unperturbed having enjoyed an overnight stop at a good hotel in Bombay at the airline's expense - whilst I had stayed at the YMCA hostel in Delhi! By the time she reached Delhi we'd missed our ongoing direct flight to Bhutan which only operated twice weekly. As it was the quickest alternative I then booked for us on an internal Air India flight to Bagdogra in West Bengal, from where it would take a three or four-hour bus journey to reach the border of Bhutan at Phuentsholing.

Once more our plans were frustrated by fog, as the Air India flight was unable to land at Bagdogra and took us on a further several hundred miles to an airport in Assam! As this is a restricted area for foreigners we were not permitted to leave the airport; so we waited in the airport lounge all day until late afternoon when our plane finally took off once more on its return leg to Delhi. Only when we were airborne, were we told by the pilot there was little hope of landing at Bagdogra as fog still persisted there! Against all the odds however we did land – the only flight to do so, but arriving so late in the day meant that all public transport to Phuentsholing had long since departed.

Whilst sitting in Assam I had noted a well-dressed Bhutanese obviously of some importance stranded with us. Waiting to meet him at Bagdogra was a chauffeur driven Toyota Land Cruiser together with his wife. I approached him and explained our predicament and he readily and kindly agreed to give us a lift to Phuentsholing. Alison and I were only too happy to sit quietly in the back for the long drive in the dark, thankful that we were actually going to arrive in Bhutan that day and without any further enforced delay. I was somewhat perturbed when on reaching Bhutan's border with India the vehicle drove right through both the Indian and Bhutanese border controls without stopping! Knowing what sticklers the Indians are for following regulations to the letter, I anticipated trouble when Alison came to leave Bhutan - I was not to be disappointed!

It was well past ten at night when we pulled up outside the best hotel in Phuentsholing where our Bhutanese VIP was obviously booked for the night. His wife turned to us and said that as she was to visit her sister in the town she would happily drop us at our destination - which was typically kind and thoughtful and the sort of help I was given on many occasions. I took the opportunity to ask what position her husband held in government, as he was obviously a person of some rank.

'O he's the King's Personal Secretary' she replied!
After a day or two to allow Alison time to recover from her

long journey, we departed in a hired Toyota to travel first to Gidakom and then on several hundred kilometres to Mongar in eastern Bhutan - where we had been invited to spend Christmas with Gottfried and Helle Riedel and their daughter. There were no maps in Bhutan but with no more than one road to choose from for any given destination, none was needed! The road across Bhutan from Thimphu in the west to Trashigang in the east, for virtually the whole of its length of several hundred miles was single track with passing places. It was still under construction and in a number of places stretches of several kilometres were as yet only a rough dirt track.

This was my first experience of driving on these somewhat frightening roads and I set out on our journey to Mongar with a certain degree of trepidation. For most of its way the route threads its way through mountains and in places the road is hewn out of sheer rock faces where there are often horrifying drops of hundreds of feet from the side. The road traverses three mountain passes of 10500 feet (3200m) and higher, and in December these are often under a good covering of snow.

All went well for the first 150 miles (240km) and we were only about 20 miles (32km) from our overnight stop in Bumthang, when without warning the car's engine cut out! There are no breakdown services in Bhutan and precious few citizens have the know-how to get you going again! How I wished that before I'd left the UK I had taken a car maintenance course at College as well as first aid! We were in the middle of nowhere and it was very dark. I peered under the bonnet to see if there was any obvious cause for engine failure - but could find nothing. Knowing that we would be stuck there in the freezing cold until daybreak otherwise, I retried the ignition after a few minutes not really expecting anything to happen. Miraculously it fired and away we went for a few more miles until then it died on us a second time. Again we waited for five or so minutes and once more the engine fired and on we travelled. After several such enforced stops and starts, we were greatly relieved to actually reach our destination for the night.

We were booked at a Guest House run by 'Helvetas'- the Swiss overseas development agency. They had been working in Bumthang in Central Bhutan since the 1960's and had established a number of projects including the Guest House - a cosy wood cabin with several bedrooms, plus communal living room, all heated by an effective wood burning stove. An outhouse boasted the ultimate luxury - a shower with an ample supply of hot water. These comforts were tempered by reality in one respect - the only toilet was a rather smelly 'pit latrine' built in a 'privy' a distance from the back of the main cabin. Helvetas had also trained up a local man as cook, who provided simple but sumptuous food for weary travellers. After a very welcome meal we slept soundly for the night in the knowledge that next day we would be travelling in a 4 x 4 vehicle that had already arrived from Mongar Hospital to fetch us - driven by a qualified car mechanic!

Bumthang Valley in Central Bhutan with Jakar Dzong on the left.

After a substantial breakfast, we continued on the final leg of our journey to Mongar - 120 miles (193 km) away. About a third of this section of road was still to be surfaced and took us over the highest road pass on this 'lateral' road, at 12300 feet (3750m) through deep snow. Here the 4 x 4 Toyota Land Cruiser really proved its worth. We had the surreal experience of driving above clouds that filled the valley below the road with an undulating blanket of fluffy white cloud.

We spent a lovely Christmas at Mongar, enjoying the hospitality of the Riedels' and sharing in some of their German traditions and a very simple communal Christmas Day meal of rice with curried pork and vegetables, served and eaten together with the hospital staff and leprosy patients, outside in warm sunshine.

At the end of the visit we were transported back to Bumthang and retrieved our hire car for the return journey to Kharbandi. The 'Helvetas' garage staff had serviced the car and for most of the day it performed well and without the engine trouble that had plagued us on the outward journey. At Wangduephodang we picked up two students wanting a lift to Thimphu. They proved to be a great asset!

Having climbed from Wangdi to around 9000 feet (2700m) towards the pass of Docha la, once again the engine decided it had had enough and cut out! Manfully, the two lads did their best to effect a 'bump start' but without success. Once more I tried the waiting game and after a few minutes the ignition fired and we climbed a few more miles before the engine cut out yet again. This happened several times and each time we were making less and less progress until finally the engine died completely! An inspection under the bonnet for any obvious fault drew a blank and laying in the snow on my back I also examined the fuel line under the car - again finding nothing amiss. 'What to do?' as the Bhutanese would say! What happened next will long be imprinted on my memory. A tourist minibus (a rare sight in those days) came by at just the right moment and seeing our predicament its kindly Bhutanese driver took our car in tow; Alison and the two students transferring to the minibus. He was obviously not used to towing and set off up the mountain road at some speed swinging round the hairpin bends as fast as he could go; whilst I, on the end of the tow rope tried desperately to steer the careering car, without hitting the rock face on one side or going off the edge of the mountain on the other! To add insult to injury the whole episode was being recorded with a video camera by a tourist hanging out of the window - who obviously thought the threat to my life on the end of a tow rope made a worthwhile contribution to her holiday memoirs!

My imminent demise was only avoided when the tow rope parted under the strain and I was able to request the bus driver to please, please, slow down! It was with great relief that I and the car reached the top of the pass unscathed! Here the bus driver (doubling as a mechanic) obligingly dived under our car bonnet and traced the problem to a clogged fuel filter. This taught me a valuable lesson and helped me avoid getting stranded in the middle of nowhere on a couple of future occasions, when in years to come I had to drive frequently to and fro across Bhutan still without the services of an AA or RAC!

There were no fancy fuel stations in Bhutan - the petrol or diesel being transported up from India and stored in well worn and rusted, reusable metal drums. The fuel was pumped manually together with any sediment that remained in the drum from its previous usage, into your vehicle! A blocked fuel filter was therefore apparently a common problem especially as diesel fuel thickens in the kind of low winter temperatures which prevail at high altitudes. Following my experience with the hire car I knew in future what to look for and how to deal with it when the problem reoccurred. Bhutan's lorry drivers have their own unique solution. Before setting off on a winter's morning they light a fire under the fuel tank! Not a practice to be recommended!

Before returning to Kharbandi, we visited the Paro Valley and walked up to view the spectacular *Taktsang* or 'Tigers Nest' Monastery located high above the valley bottom and built hundreds of feet up near the top of a sheer rock face. The monastery is so named because legend has it that Padma Sambhava who brought Buddhism to Bhutan in 747 AD flew here from Tibet on the back of a tiger. The people believe that if you make a pilgrimage to Taktsang several times during your present lifetime, it ensures a favourable reincarnation in the next.

We reached Taktsang after walking for about three hours up a steep winding track through ranks of fluttering prayer flags. You cannot but marvel at the incredible devotion and the enormous difficulty in building such a place as this, high up on a narrow shelf of rock above a sheer precipice. The path became progressively narrower, until the final approach was across a rock face on a ledge just wide enough for one person. A waterfall made the path even more treacherous at this juncture; as a stream tumbling almost vertically down the cliff face flowed under a stone slab bridge that led to the monastery and made the path very slippery from its spray. I was amazed to see a Dipper searching for food in the waterfall, working its way up and plunging in and out of the stream. I wondered why this bird would choose to live so high up and in such an exposed place when there was much better and easier feeding in the more moderate conditions in the river flowing in the valley below.

In a spot above the path and completely isolated, was a tiny hut some way from the main monastery. It is here I understand that monks go into solitary confinement to meditate for a period of three years, three months, three weeks and three days, in their search for spiritual enlightenment. They have no contact with anybody during that time - their food being brought and left outside by other monks. I could not imagine what it must be like in solitary, cut off from all fellow human contact for almost forty months!

All too soon Alison's three-week visit came to an end and we started out on our journey back to Delhi, for her return flight to Britain. As anticipated, when we reached the Indian border post at Phuentsholing, the border guard looked in our passports in vain and with growing irritation, for the entry showing our passage from India into Bhutan in the first place - which of course was not there!

"When did you arrive in Bhutan?" He asked.

I gave him our date of arrival about three weeks previous.

"And what was your place of entry"?

"Phuentsholing" I answered as innocently as possible.

"But there is no record of your arrival in your passports," he countered.

I explained - "Well it was rather difficult, as we arrived late at night in a private vehicle that didn't stop at the border". He then showed every sign of bringing the full force of his authority to bear, as the pitch of his voice was noticeably raised and his head shook from side to side! "No matter what time you arrive, it is absolutely mandatory to report at this check point and to have your passports stamped to show that you are leaving India," he said, in a rather officious manner. I decided the time had arrived to play my trump card.

"Well, you see," I explained, "it was rather awkward as we were travelling with the King of Bhutan's Private Secretary!"

There was a pregnant pause.

"O, I see!" He responded.

At which point after the briefest thoughtful pause, he turned the date stamp back three weeks, recorded our leaving India, turned it forward again to the current date, and duly recorded our re-entry into India! Three weeks compressed into three minutes! This must be an all time record for Indian bureaucracy! (It was not the last time that pulling Royal strings was to get me out of potentially awkward situations!) Somewhat relieved, Alison and I proceeded on our way, having momentarily suffered visions of languishing in an Indian prison until such time as we were missed by someone!

As we said our goodbyes, Alison had no notion that three years later she would be returning to live in Bhutan to take up a post with the Leprosy Mission at Gidakom Hospital and Bhutan would be her home for more than seven years.

Chapter 7

An IMAGINATIVE and UNUSUAL REWARD

As an expression of thanks for the work being done by volunteers, in January of 1986 the Education Department arranged and financed a trek for us into the heart of the Himalaya's. This imaginative way of rewarding us for our service was open to any volunteer teacher who wished to avail themselves of it. The final party of eighteen – came from Britain, Ireland, Canada and New Zealand, and we were accompanied by four Bhutanese helpers. Everything (or nearly everything) was meticulously thought out for the trek, which was planned to last just over a week. It was all provided for by the Royal Government; including a guide, a cook, pack mules, mule drivers, tents and food. We had only to take a rucksack for our own personal items such as sleeping bag, toiletries and clothing and even this was actually carried for us on the pack animals from one overnight stop to the next.

The trek took us further north and to a higher altitude than I had ever been before, and we were surrounded all the way by the most magnificent pristine scenery. Being January and midwinter in Bhutan it was extremely cold at night, but during the day, most days, the sun shone out of the deepest of deep blue sky. The ground was largely snow and ice covered and in places quite treacherous. The river we followed was also mostly frozen over and added to the spectacular nature of the Himalayan landscape.

Our adventure began at the head of the Paro Valley near the ruin of the ancient fortified Drugyel Dzong - built centuries ago to repel invasions by the Tibetans from the north. Near the old Dzong the metalled road ended and three days of trekking following the Paro Chu River north most of the way, would lead us to the base of 'Jichudrakey', one of Bhutan's highest mountains bordering Tibet.

Though the most careful planning and thorough provisioning had gone into providing for our every need for the duration of the trek; at the end of the first day and not many kilometres from the start we met with a seemingly insurmountable problem! Getting past the Bhutanese army check post where all travellers on this route are vetted! Apparently the route was used by smugglers to cross the border into Tibet, returning with all manner of illegal contraband from rice bowls to electric torches. The small yet vital administrative detail of notifying the army that a motley group of foreigners would be passing through this strategic check post had unfortunately been overlooked!

In Bhutan there is a well-established hierarchical structure of government, very strict protocol and an ingrained respect for authority. Proceeding without securing the necessary authorisation was out of the question and a lengthy discussion took place between our guide and the army commander - but without resolving the issue of obtaining the permission required to continue on our journey. Feeling most frustrated to be halted by what we saw as a bit of bureaucratic nonsense, we had little choice but to take the unwelcome hold-up in good part and wait patiently for the permit to be obtained. So we pitched our first camp amid falling snow within sight of the army base and there we waited. Getting the vital piece of paper was not as straight forward as one might think, as telecommunications in Bhutan was still very much in its infancy! A frantic dash during the night all the way to Thimphu and back by an army officer in person, was necessary to obtain the required paper work.

We slept two to a tent, in quite spacious if rather old fashioned bell tents fitted with an integral ground sheet and pitched for us by our Bhutanese helpers. It was far too cold to undress at night so we slid fully clothed inside our sleeping bags, only divesting ourselves of walking boots! By the morning the inside of the tent was covered in a thin layer of ice formed from freezing breath - and our walking boots were frozen solid!

At seven thirty in the morning we were awakened with a cup of steaming hot 'bed tea' served through the flap of the tent - what a luxury! This was followed at eight thirty by an amazing full cooked breakfast, served on trestle tables inside a mess tent where we sat on seats along either side. Breakfast began with a choice of porridge or grapefruit segments, followed by fried egg, sausage, fried bread and baked beans. It was rounded off with buttered toast and the excellent 'Druk' marmalade and all washed down with an ample supply of coffee. This full English-style cooked breakfast was repeated every morning of the trek and set us up for each new day ahead. It was staggering service, especially considering that all the food and equipment for the complete trek had to be carried on mules from the start; that the cooking was all done on open fires, and none of us as 'guests' were expected to lift a finger to help – or wash up afterwards! I was even provided each morning with a mug of piping hot water to shave with!

To our delight and relief, after just the one night here under canvas, by morning the required clearance to proceed had been obtained! Before setting off the following day we were all issued with packed lunches plus a large can of fruit juice to be shared between two - and a tin opener! When we left camp, all the tents were still standing, the campfire was still burning and the unladen ponies were still quietly munching from their nose bags. Around midday, the heavily laden ponies with all the gear firmly tied to their backs, together with their drivers, would pass by us travelling at a rapid rate of knots, soon to disappear up ahead. By the time we reached our next camp site at the end of the day's trek; the tents would be already pitched, a log fire already burning and a welcome cup of tea waiting! Our willing Bhutanese helpers certainly knew how to provide a service - and all with a warm smile and obvious and genuine pleasure that we were being enabled to share the magnificent scenery of their country!

The first full day of trekking followed the Paro Chu - the major river that flows down through the Paro Valley, toward its source at a glacier somewhere distant in the high Himalaya to the north. It was treacherous walking in places as much of the route was under freshly fallen snow which hid the icy ground and ice covered rocks beneath. The ponies struggled and had difficulty keeping their feet in the treacherous conditions, laden as they were with all our baggage and the camping equipment.

The river was mostly ice and each boulder was fringed with icicles frozen in all manner of weird and wonderful shapes. Water only ran in the very middle of the river where the rate of flow was too great to allow it to freeze completely. On the first day, the surrounding mountain sides were partly forested and in places the trail was forced to divert away from the river bank due to rock-falls. Where this had happened, the route would deviate for a short distance up through the forest skirting the obstruction, before dropping back again to follow the river bank once more. We crossed several tributaries on bridges constructed simply out of huge horizontal logs laid with a decking of planks. These were also encrusted in ice and snow and had to be crossed with great care.

Periodically we were reminded that Bhutan is a deeply devout Buddhist country: as even in this seemingly uninhabited and remote frozen wilderness the route was marked at intervals by rows of tattered prayer flags; or by small stone memorial structure's known as *'chortens'* – built around some significant holy relic; and occasionally the trail would skirt a prayer or *'mani'* wall, on which the Buddhist mantra, was inscribed in slate inlaid along the length of the wall, repeated over and over again, along both sides. This is read from right to left, so such prayer walls were always passed on one's right side. To facilitate this; throughout Bhutan any path, track or road, on reaching a prayer wall always divides into two, passing down both sides of the wall before merging into one again; so in whichever direction you are travelling the mantra can be read.

After our first full day of trekking and having covered about 11 miles (18 km), we camped for the night under a clear star studded sky on an open piece of ground surrounded by pine trees. We were treated to an evening camp meal 'a la Bhutanese', and once again it was amazing to see what was achievable on an open fire! A three course meal materialised - starting with soup, followed by a main course of chicken with rice and vegetables and completed with a dessert of tinned fruit served with cream. It was nicely rounded off with coffee. (It would never have surprised me had our Bhutanese cooks-come-carers, handed round the port and the after dinner mints!)

The next day dawned bright and sunny and after a repeat performance of the rising and breakfasting routine with the same impeccable level of service, we set out on the next leg. After wending our way through pine forest, (in which we were intrigued to see a single wire following us along the route strung up like a washing line between slender poles), we came to a more open landscape. In the middle distance, majestic towering snow covered mountaintops could be seen; whilst flanking us on both sides, were steep snow slopes stretching up to dramatic peaks that seemed almost directly above us.

Part way through the afternoon we reached a large, well-built stone and log cabin sited right alongside our route. Here the mysterious and intriguing single wire that we had followed all day, terminated. Two smartly dressed Indian Army officers appeared as if by magic and persuasively shepherded us in, insisting we join them for afternoon tea! They spoke with cultured 'Sandhurst' accents and were so eager to engage us in conversation - so that afterwards no doubt they could complete their intelligence report as to what this motley group of westerners was doing so close to the Tibetan border! I gained the distinct impression that in this far flung outpost, any visitor was a rarity and native English speakers almost unheard of! I wondered if this was Bhutan's equivalent of 'Fylingdales' in Yorkshire - the early warning system should trouble arise on this sensitive border with Tibet. Both officers were athletic looking - selected (perhaps) so they could outrun the Chinese should they ever breach the border! After this quite unexpected interlude of afternoon tea and biscuits served with some panache on a china tea service, we eventually said goodbye feeling rather sorry for these two hospitable and gregarious soldiers, holed up out here in isolation for who knows how many months at a time - with just a field telephone for company.

From the very start of our trek the route had been steadily, though almost imperceptibly rising as it followed the Paro Chu River toward its source. We must have now reached an altitude exceeding 10,000 feet and began to encounter the first yak herds and the occasional solitary yak herder's cabin. It must be an incredibly lonely and difficult existence for these men and their families, living in the middle of nowhere in such an uncompromisingly harsh environment but a life no doubt they have been brought up to.

Yaks are massive shaggy animals with dangerous looking horns and they have a reputation for being somewhat unpredictable and sometimes aggressive. They are mainly kept for milk production from which butter and cheese is made, as well as being used as pack animals. The yak herders being Buddhists will not deliberately kill an animal for its meat but if a yak dies either naturally or by accident, then the meat, skin and hair, etc. is all utilised. Nothing is wasted.

Toward the end of that afternoon I found a young yak calf frozen on its knees and unable to move. Our Bhutanese guide brought the plight of the animal to the attention of the yak herder and his wife and with some difficulty, between the four of us we carried it into the herdsman's hut where it could recover. The couple was so pleased to have saved the animal that would probably have died without our intervention; they pressed us to accept a string of yak cheese or *'chugo'* as a gift.

Chugo is a product I had seen for sale in Thimphu market but not knowing what it was had never tried it. It resembles pieces of fudge threaded on a string like a necklace and is the Bhutanese equivalent of a packet of chewing gum! One lozenge at a time of the hard and very solid yak cheese is unthreaded and chewed, and chewed, and chewed - it seems to last for ever! Eventually it chews to nothing so unlike chewing gum does not leave unsightly sticky deposits on pavements - were there pavements that is. Maybe there's an export opportunity for chugo to replace chewing gum in the west!

As we steadily gained in altitude so the air became thinner and breathing became noticeably more laboured, yet because the climb was a very gradual one none of our group suffered ill effects from altitude sickness. However, walking did become more of an effort as we gained height, so gradually our pace slowed. Our Bhutanese companions seemed to suffer no such adverse effects and appeared as energetic and inexhaustible as ever - the pony handlers continuing to pass us around midday still going at twice our pace! Also as we gained altitude, though the sun shone it grew noticeably colder and the snow on the ground changed from being just a partial covering to a total blanket. The only thing that moved in the frozen landscape beside us was the yak, as they patiently foraged for what they could find to eat under the snow.

Having walked a total of 14 miles (22 km) that day, we reached the site where we would camp for our third night - in a barren frozen landscape surrounded by towering, awesome, ice covered mountains. The tents were pitched almost in the back garden of another yak herder's cabin. After yet another amazing three course dinner out under the stars with a blazing camp fire going, it was with reluctance that we eventually retired to our tents to sleep. During the night the outdoor temperature sank to minus 27 degrees Celsius (one of our party actually carried a thermometer) and it was not the best night to take a trip to the bathroom (joking of course), but just to see the amazing night sky adorned with countless stars, for me was well worth risking frostbite! By the time the next day dawned we were in especial need of that welcome cup of steaming hot bed tea. The tent walls on the inside were a sheet of ice and our walking boots - frozen solid, were unyielding and very difficult to get on!

The guide learned from the yak herders that deep snow, fallen the previous night, now totally blocked the pass ahead and it might well remain impassable for some days to come. This was the only way forward, so it was now impossible to proceed much further north on our intended route. This turn of events made us feel better able to accept with good grace, our enforced return to Paro by the same route as that taken on our outward journey.

At Jhomolhari Base Camp – author on far left.

Just to the north was Jhomolhari - 23990 feet (7314m), one of Bhutan's highest mountains with the ruins of an ancient fortress and watch tower at its base.

The morning was just perfect and because of our altitude the sky was a deeper blue than I had ever seen before. I had a wonderful feeling of wellbeing and the air was crisp and dry to breathe. Newly fallen snow crunched and sparkled underfoot. As we explored further to the north the top of Jhomolhari was visible for most of the way and as we headed up the valley, more and more of the mountain was gradually revealed as we neared its base.

Even this close it was difficult to grasp the scale of the mountain, the top of which was still more than 10 000 feet (3000m) above us. The whole of Jhomolhari presented a gleaming pyramid of snow and ice with just a wisp of white wind drift snow trailing from its summit against the deep azure blue of the sky. We were now just a few miles from the Tibetan border – and the far side of Jhomolhari was in Tibet. Our group stopped to pose for a photo against the dramatic backdrop of the mountain with the ancient ruined fortress in the background and then some of us made our way further north to within sight of the next spectacular peak of 'Jichudrakey'. Though not so high at 22284 feet (6794m), Jichudrakey has an immense near vertical face of ice, which towered up many thousands of feet to its summit from the valley in which we stood.

Unable to go any further north on the intended route to the village of Lingshi due to the depth of snow blocking the pass; with some reluctance at this point we now turned back to begin trekking south again toward Paro.

It was inevitable that in the course of a day the group would get spread out in one's and two's and on that first day of our return journey one member of our group walking on her own, had an experience that made the rest of us very envious. She had stopped to take a breather and was leant against a large boulder idly looking across the frozen river to the far bank, when she saw part of the snow move, get up and walk! It was a pair of snow leopards that had been laid on the bank opposite - perfectly camouflaged - until they moved that is! Some of our party must have passed them by un-noticed! When she reached camp she couldn't contain her excitement as she told us of her encounter. The snow leopard is an extremely rare animal, found only in the high Himalaya and very seldom seen, especially at such close quarters.

My own encounter that day was of a very different kind but

one that also caused me to marvel. I met an old man walking on the same path but in the opposite direction. While he was still some way off, it was clear that he was moving rather slowly and with great care - with the aid of a staff. As we drew closer to one another I was astounded to see that he was blind and feeling his way along this icy path with only his stick to aid him. It was one of those occasions when I would have liked to have been able to speak Dzongkha; to ask him how far he had come and whether he was hoping to travel to Lingshi. Had his blindness I wondered, been caused by walking in such conditions without eye protection - snow blindness? It just amazed me how any blind person could cope alone on such a rough path through hostile and potentially dangerous terrain in mid winter!

As we journeyed south the clear weather gave way to snow showers which transformed our surroundings into a wonder land. The trees - bedecked all year round with long strands of lichen were now also covered with fresh snow. When the sun shone the lichen was transformed into countless necklaces threaded with tiny sparkling jewelled droplets along their length. As we progressed further south we reached a more cultivated area with the occasional farmhouse - built in the lovely traditional style rather than the roughly built unadorned stone dwellings of the yak herders. These houses reminded me so much of Swiss chalets with their large overhanging roofs and attractive timbering.

Right to the end of the trek we were treated to the same unvarying and cheerful high level of service we had enjoyed from the beginning. After more than a week spent together we were really getting to know Jigme our guide and his team of willing helpers. On the last night we entertained one another in community singing; the men engaged in arm wrestling and the mule drivers indulged in a masculine show of bravado leaping through the flames of a huge camp fire.

We were all rather sad that our adventure was coming to its end. Though we had endured the harshest walking conditions that most if not all of us had ever experienced; and the lowest temperatures any of us had certainly ever slept out in; we had all thoroughly enjoyed the experience of trekking through some of the most awesome and dramatic scenery in the world. We'd been looked after with incredible devotion and cheerfulness and were unanimous in the view that the Education Department could not have chosen a better or more imaginative way to express their thanks; than in gifting to us such a wonderful wilderness experience – one I am sure none of us will ever forget.

Chapter 8

A Right Royal Response

It was a very exciting day for staff and students when we learned of the intended visit to Kharbandi College of the King of Bhutan for the very first time in his reign. A Royal visit that was to prove extra special for me in a most unexpected way!

At just 32 years of age, King Jigme Singye Wangchuck, ruler of the Kingdom of Bhutan was the youngest monarch in the world and the fourth king in succession since the Bhutanese monarchy was declared in 1907 to unify what had been for centuries a fragmented and feudal society. The King of Bhutan has the title *'Druk Gyalpo'* - 'Precious Ruler of the Dragon People'; Bhutan being *'Druk Yul'* - 'Land of the Thunder Dragon'!

When I first went to work in Bhutan, I quickly learned that the King was in no way simply a constitutional figurehead but very definitely the ruler of His Kingdom. He was a monarch who still exercised considerable power over his subjects. Not only did he take important decisions of state on how the country should be run and administered; but like Solomon of Old Testament fame he might also intervene in disputes of a purely personal nature concerning one of his subjects and decide how it should be resolved. I heard various stories from my Bhutanese colleagues that underlined the power that their monarch wielded and was left in no doubt of the very high regard, indeed almost awe, in which he was held. Several of the staff at Kharbandi, had in fact been servers at the King's coronation twelve years beforehand on the 2nd June 1974. When the news broke that His Majesty was to make this very first and totally unexpected visit to Kharbandi College, there was considerable speculation among the staff as to what His purpose might be? Was it simply to see the facilities and training or might there be some less obvious and more sinister reason? Could it be perhaps to admonish staff for some misdeed that had been brought to his notice? They were obviously concerned and worked hard to make sure that everything was as ready as it could be for His visit. For some weeks beforehand there was much careful planning, rehearsal, and 'spit and polish', to prepare staff, students and the campus for the occasion.

Several weeks before His Majesty was due one of his aides arrived, to put everyone including myself through a course of Bhutanese Royal etiquette - or *'Driglam Namzha'*. We were all required to wear the national dress - which for men is a dense, beautifully hand woven long robe-like garment called a *'kho'* or *'boku'*. This wraps around the body and is hitched up with a narrow tightly wound belt at the waist, so that it is held just above the knee and rather resembles a Scottish kilt. It has broad full length sleeves and a plain white cotton garment worn inside the kho, is turned back over the sleeves to form wide white (or off white if it's not been washed) cuffs. Above the waist the ample fold in the kho forms a most useful pouch; used to stow virtually anything you wish to carry, from potatoes to personal items like comb, handkerchief or lecture notes! It is the most difficult garment imaginable to put on properly - single handed. Bhutanese men normally enlist the help of their wives to ensure that their kho's hang properly - perfectly level front and back. Of course for the King's visit every one on campus had to be dressed immaculately, so when the big day came I enlisted Dawa and Pema my two ever willing helpers, to assist me in dressing for the occasion.

In addition to wearing the national dress, we were instructed at length by the King's aide in the use of a ceremonial scarf or 'kabney' - worn as a mark of respect. We were taught how to approach and then how to withdraw from the King's presence without turning your back on him, bent over almost double at the waist and facing the ground.

Strict protocol governed everything that could and couldn't be done during the visit. The staff wanted a photographic record of this auspicious occasion and as I was a keen photographer and owned the only camera, I was asked to take the photos; provided that is, His Majesty granted the necessary permission! Apparently the King was generally not over keen on having his photograph taken! On the evening before the royal visit a member of staff was duly dispatched to the King's overnight quarters, to request through the proper channels consent for photographs to be taken. Permission was granted, so I made quite sure my camera and film was 'ready' to record his visit for posterity.

Next day the first sign of His Majesty's imminent arrival was when several army trucks drove on to the campus full of the King's bodyguards. Well armed, the guards dispersed to key positions all round the grounds in a most impressive show of force and efficiency. The King then arrived in His gleaming Toyota Land Cruiser together with his Personal Bodyguard; followed by the Lord Chief Justice of Bhutan (the King's uncle) and the Minister of Education in their own 4 x 4 Toyota's.

All the staff including myself was lined up in readiness along one side of the basketball court to receive His Majesty - the Bhutanese waiting with some apprehension to discover whether they were to be admonished, or praised, or what! They are not meant to look directly at their King and the Bhutanese staff members gazed steadfastly at the ground whilst he addressed them, but as he spoke in Dzongkha I was blissfully ignorant of what he was saying. When the King spoke to any individual and they were expected to give a reply, they did so with head bowed and eyes down; talking quietly down the sleeve of their kho to ensure that *even their breath* did not fall on His Majesty. As a westerner and a sort of 'guest' in Bhutan I did not feel so bound by the restrictions of protocol and while he was talking managed to sneak the first photograph without it being too obvious! The King then moved to the other side of the basketball court to address the student body that were assembled there. They gazed even more earnestly at the ground while the King addressed them at some length from under the shade of a large umbrella held by his uniformed Personal Bodyguard. I sneaked another photo.

His Majesty at just thirty-two had already ruled for some twelve years so much of his adult life had been spent surrounded by the trappings of power - and body guards! It was widely known that the King had a passion for basketball so when his duties allowed, he would play as often as possible with his guards in order to keep fit. So the next part of the programme was obviously decided on by the King. A basketball match was to be played between a team consisting of the King himself, the Lord Chief Justice, his Personal Bodyguard and several others of his guards - against our regular college team. The newly - appointed Minister of Education sat next to me at the side of the court. He was not at all keen on basketball and sat through the game in fear and trembling, fully expecting that any moment he would be summoned to join in! Our student team had the very real handicap of playing against His Majesty whilst not appearing to be too aggressive, or obviously looking him in the face - so His Majesty's team won, just! During the match I was able to sneak a few more photos.

The match put everyone at ease and then the King plus his Ministers and aids took a tour of the workshops to observe our students at work. I duly followed at what I thought was a discreet distance taking more pictures, knowing how they would be greatly prized and treasured, especially by individuals who the King stopped to talk to.

Part way through the workshop tour, one of His Majesty's aides came over to me and said politely but firmly, 'That was enough photos and I should not take any more!' After touring all of the college facilities, the King and the Education Minister were closeted with the Principal in his office for some time for private discussions and light refreshment. When eventually they emerged, I was requested to take an official group photo of the King together with the Principal and other Officials at the entrance to the college. Apparently this concluded his official visit, and the King started to walk toward his Land Cruiser and the bodyguards moved in preparation to depart the campus in convoy with him. The other members of the entourage began to board their own vehicles.

Midway between the front steps of the college and his vehicle the King suddenly turned and walked directly toward me. Whilst I was wondering what on earth was going to happen next, without a word he took my camera gave it to his personal bodyguard, ordering him to take a photograph of the two of us; just the King and I stood side by side in front of the college! I was taken completely by surprise and absolutely lost for words! Once the picture had been taken the bodyguard returned my camera to me; without comment or further ado the King boarded his Land Cruiser and the convoy moved off. After he had left, the staff told me just how unusual it was for His Majesty to be photographed with any one individual in this way! So I felt very honoured and privileged indeed.

King Jigme Singye Wangchuk and the Author

In later years I had to travel regularly from one district of Bhutan to another, passing through various police check posts. Stuck inside the back cover of my passport I always carried a small print of that prized photograph of the King and me. It assured me of a smooth passage without delay or questions - as every Bhutanese, whether or not they are literate immediately recognises their King – and even if they don't know who on earth the stranger is that is stood beside him, he must surely be of some importance!

110

Not long after the King made this first visit to Kharbandi College it was announced that in future it was to be known as 'The Royal Technical Institute' as the King wanted the key role the college had to play in the future development of Bhutan to be more widely recognised and appreciated. This was a proud moment for the staff at Kharbandi and a great boost to their morale. The apprehension they had felt prior to that first visit had proved groundless and the staff could not have wished for a more resounding endorsement of all their hard work in the training of Bhutan's future technical personnel.

A few months later the King visited again to have talks with the new British Principal, Denis Lee. At the end of the visit His Majesty kindly offered that if Denis and family would like to tour across Bhutan at His expense he would personally authorise that it be arranged. It was an offer few would or could refuse and in accepting Denis kindly requested that I be included in the party - and His Majesty agreed. The very next day one of the King's aides came to make detailed arrangements for the future trip.

It was a trip I eagerly looked forward to, as it afforded a wonderful opportunity to visit parts of Bhutan that I had not seen and imagined I would probably never have the opportunity to see otherwise. Two days before we were due to set off on this trip of a lifetime, as I lifted a bowl of water out of the kitchen sink I felt a stabbing pain in my lower back and knew immediately I had displaced a disc in my lower spine. It was not the first time I'd suffered a 'slipped' disc, so I knew only too well that the way to recover was to rest flat on my back until it went back into place and that this usually took a week or two! With all the detailed arrangements for the tour in place it was not possible at this late stage to change them without causing considerable disruption and embarrassment; so to my immense disappointment the Lee family had to leave without me, and another VSO Michael Reed, went in my place.

The two weeks I should have been touring Bhutan at the Kings expense, I spent flat on my back being wonderfully cared for by my neighbours, who provided meals and generally looked after me superbly; but I determined then and there that should it prove possible, before I returned to Britain for good, I would arrange my own grand tour across Bhutan.

Near the end of my initial two-year contract to teach at Kharbandi I was requested to extend my service for a further year. As I now knew something of the social and cultural background of the country as well as the college and its needs, I agreed. After an eventful ten week break in Britain over the summer of 1986 catching up with family and friends, I returned once again to teach at The Royal Technical Institute.

Like many in the 'western world'; at home in Britain I had owned a car for years and enjoyed the independence that that gave me. Being without personal transport in Bhutan I had found somewhat limiting so when I returned, I took with me sufficient funds to buy an Indian Bajaj motor scooter. This proved to be a resilient and reliable machine that gave to me just the degree of freedom I was looking for; to get down to the local market for fresh food when I wanted, or to travel up to Gidakom or Thimphu without having to book a seat and suffer the discomfort of travelling on the public bus - the 'vomit comet'!

So it was that on completion of that additional third year of teaching and before I returned home for good (or so I thought), it became possible to embark upon my own grand tour of Bhutan on my Bajaj scooter. It was unfortunate that the end of my contract coincided with the onset of the monsoon - the very worst time to travel on Bhutan's roads, but as there was no choice in the matter I decided to make the trip anyway!

Chapter 9

Bhutan by Motor Scooter – Western Bhutan

My journey across Bhutan in July/August of 1987 was not made at the King's expense and not in the comfort of a Land Cruiser but I think I can claim that it was probably the first ever crossing of Bhutan on a motor scooter! The only road going east-west across country takes you over three formidable mountain passes, the highest at 12,300 feet (3750m), and the complete return trip would cover more than a thousand miles. Unfortunately, as my contract finished at the end of July it was the worst possible time of the year to make the journey as it could be very wet and the road was often blocked by land slides - sometimes for weeks; all-in-all it would turn out to be quite an adventure.

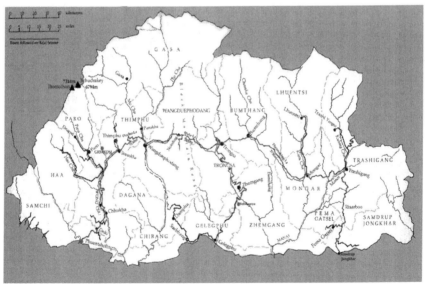

Route across Bhutan by Motor Scooter shown in red - a return journey of over a thousand miles.

Wherever possible I planned to stay with people I knew; who

were either teaching with VSO or working in hospitals with the Leprosy Mission. Exactly when I might arrive at any particular place and for how long I might stay there was left rather open-ended, as everyone appreciated, that travelling on Bhutan's roads during monsoon was a haphazard and uncertain affair; even when travelling in a 4 x 4 let alone on a humble motor scooter!

Riding by scooter is a great way to travel. You can stop and park when you want, to admire the scenery or take photographs, or just to take a break when you feel like it. A scooter doesn't make much noise, especially in Bhutan; as for half your journey you're coasting downhill with the ignition switched off! Though illegal in Britain, it was an absolute necessity in Bhutan to get from one refuelling point to the next. Fuel stations were so far apart that even with the main and emergency tanks full to the brim, there was still insufficient fuel to drive from one depot to the next if the engine was kept running the whole time! On the plus side, the little or no engine noise when coasting - had the advantage of greatly increasing your chance of seeing wildlife.

The main disadvantage on a scooter is you have no protection whatever against the weather! Monsoon conditions can be absolutely atrocious - like driving underwater; which I was to discover to my cost on the return leg of the journey. The other major drawback is that you are much less visible and therefore much more vulnerable, than if travelling in an enclosed vehicle! I had to exercise great care driving on Bhutan's roads as being almost all virtually single track; you never knew what you might meet head-on around the next bend! You had to always be alert in anticipating people, animals, as well as vehicles possibly blocking the road around the next blind corner.

However, in 1987 there was still little traffic on Bhutan's roads compared to most other countries and especially on the east to west lateral road which I would be travelling on for most of the journey. The busiest section by far would be the 105 miles (170 km) from Phuentsholing to Thimphu; along which all Bhutan's imported supplies including their fuel has to be transported. However, this part was familiar to me as I had made the journey by scooter to Gidakom several times already - a reasonable day's drive of around six hours.

As I set out from Kharbandi on my 'Grand Tour of Bhutan' it was sunny and dry and the first leg was achieved easily without incident and I arrived at Gidakom well before evening. I stayed there for several days, as from this base I could conveniently travel into Thimphu: to obtain the travel permits at Tashichho Dzong that I needed for my journey to the far east; to collect mail from the VSO Field Office for the volunteers that I would be seeing on route; as well as to stock up on a few food items for the journey.

When all these preparations were in place I left Gidakom early one morning on the next, and rather more demanding leg of the journey. Packed into the small metal panniers built under the seat of the scooter and in a rucksack strapped on my back, I carried the very barest essentials for the trip. It helped a lot, that the past three years had taught me to manage with very few possessions! I was mindful that within about an hour of setting out, I would be crossing the mountain pass of Dochu la at 10 332 feet (3150 m) and I was not at all sure how the scooter would function at this altitude. I was also concerned to reach my next overnight stop at

Punakha before dark and I had no idea of the state of the road that led there, not having driven that way before.

I need not have worried! The scooter behaved perfectly as it laboured its way up the 1800 feet (550m) climb from the Thimphu Valley to the top of Dochu la in the space of just a few miles - carrying my (then) 175 pounds (80 kilos) body weight plus a full rucksack and a full fuel tank; without any trouble at all! The top of the pass was enveloped in mist and the valleys and forest slopes stretching down from the top were also wreathed in cloud and mist. The many prayer flags, a *'mani'* wall and a large chorten, which mark the top of Dochula, took shape rather eerily out of the mist as if suspended in mid air. On the top it was perfectly still and silent, apart from the drip, drip of water from the huge rhododendron bushes along the side of the road, their wet leaves shining iridescently as they caught the light. In winter, when the atmosphere is clear and crisp this pass affords a wonderful vista of the mountains of the Himalaya extending to the north and east as far as the eye can see. This morning, sadly, I could see very little.

From the top of Dochula it was downhill for around 15 miles (25 km) - coasting of course! Drifting silently down and down, passing small clusters of typical Bhutanese houses surrounded by lush green terraced rice fields, and down still further to the expansive and fertile valley of Wangduephodang. This valley being at a much lower altitude than Thimphu enjoys an almost tropical climate, and its wide alluvial valley floor is covered with fertile fields, fringed in places with giant yellow flowering cacti bushes.

Typical village - passed on the way down from the Dochula pass.

A fairly good and relatively level road following the river bank branched off to the north from the main road, carrying me for several kilometres the whole of the way to the small 'town' and Dzong at Punakha. Its massive Dzong incorporates an important monastery and is built at the confluence of two rivers, the Pho Chu and Mo Chu. Up until 1960 this was the winter seat of Bhutan's government and the winter residence of the main monk body in preference to Thimphu. This is because Punakha enjoys a remarkably mild climate during the winter months in contrast to the extreme cold of Thimphu. Now that Thimphu had a reliable electricity supply it meant life there was rather more bearable in winter, so the government no longer took up temporary winter quarters in Punakha. A number of times following particularly heavy monsoon rain, the glacial lakes feeding the two rivers that converge on Punakha have burst their banks; sending torrents of mud and water down the valley, sweeping away everything in its path. Consequently, Punakha Dzong has been severely damaged several times by floodwater.

One of Bhutan's few secondary schools was in this small town (hardly a hamlet by our standards) – serving pupils from a large area. I stayed the night here with a teacher with VSO who I had never actually met before. Everyone working with VSO gave hospitality to other volunteers passing through, whether or not they had fore-warning of a visit. In the absence of any telephone service such unexpected visitors at least provided the host with a welcome opportunity to catch up on news of colleagues working elsewhere; provide a chance to exchange experiences and discuss problems; and receive the eagerly-awaited personal mail from the VSO office in Thimphu.

As a visitor you might have to sleep on the floor depending on what the accommodation was like, and you took pot luck as to any food that might be on offer. In many of the remoter VSO postings to primary schools, food supplies were not easily obtained and just getting the bare essentials to live could be difficult. Because I was based so near to the market in Phuentsholing I could buy treats such as cheese and chocolate to take with me when visiting as such luxuries were simply unobtainable in many places 'inland'.

It was always interesting to compare the situations of other volunteers to your own. I quickly discovered that I was very well accommodated compared to many. A few teachers had no option but to endure very basic living conditions indeed,

119

because there was simply nothing better to be had anywhere in the place they were teaching. Bhutanese houses are very attractive to look at but the vast majority had no direct water supply, no electricity, no toilet, in fact no mod cons whatsoever. One fellow teacher asked my advice as to how she could prevent mice and rats from entering her quarters! Wire wool scouring pads proved to be the most effective material for blocking rat holes!

A communal bath in the open air and in full public view would be used by all of the inhabitants of a village. Supplied with water from a nearby stream, the bath water is heated with boulders taken from a fire built alongside the tub - the original 'immersion' heater! When the wooden tub is full and ready for action, all the villagers might take a bath one after the other; the water constantly reheated by dropping in further hot stones as required. You can imagine the fascination of the villagers never having seen a westerner before, watching the newly appointed foreign primary school teacher with 'pink' skin; take his or her bath in public for the first time! Imagine your dilemma as a VSO faced with the difficult choice of either taking a bath in public with the whole village looking on, or going without one for months on end!

Leaving Punakha after just one night and shortly after rejoining the main road, I crossed over the Punak Chu River on a steel 'Bailey' bridge (a replacement for a traditional cantilever bridge that had been swept away by floodwaters in 1968). The planking forming the roadway looked as if it had been in continuous service since 1968! It had numerous large holes in it just waiting to swallow the tiny front wheel of the scooter should I let my attention wander for a split second! Having crossed the bridge safely I was now in the district of

Wangduephodang (Wangdi for short). It's impressive Dzong visible high above the river is built in a fine defensive position crowning the top of a steep cliff and stands several hundred feet above the confluence of two rivers. The road ahead zigzagged steeply up from the bridge, until at the top I entered a bazaar of single-storey ramshackle shops stretched out along one side of the road – which was Wangdi. Across open ground to my left opposite the shops, was its vital fuel station - my last chance to fill up the Bajaj until Trongsa – another 80 miles (129 km) away!

Courtyard inside Wangduephodang Dzong

Just off the main square is the imposing entrance to Wangduephodang Dzong; decorated with traditional Buddhist paintings portraying cosmic mandala and representations of the various reincarnations of the Guru Rimpoche who had first brought Buddhism to Bhutan in the eighth century AD. Such paintings were still used to teach the largely illiterate population the basic tenets of Buddhism. The Dzong entrance led into a large and imposing courtyard surrounded by a massive double-storey timbered building with a covered veranda all round at ground level. Bhutanese can only enter a Dzong or its offices if they are properly attired in the national dress - the *kho* for men and the *kira* for women; together with a ceremonial scarf worn over the shoulder - a *kabney* for men and a *raichu* for women. Foreigners visiting a Dzong are treated with understanding but are still expected to conform to a respectful dress sense.

In the square at Wangdi there was a Buddhist layman or *'manip'* dressed in the red cloak of a monk as well as a pointed red hat with gold edging. In his right hand he was rotating a prayer wheel – a common sight throughout Bhutan; but he was standing in front of an amazing portable shrine rested on top of a box the size of a tea chest in which it was obviously transported. The portable shrine, the like of which I had never seen before, is known as a *'tashigomang'* and is a complicated structure, having many doors and openings of different sizes leading into various small compartments containing statues and paintings of the Buddha. On the very top was a small statue of the Guru Rimpoche sitting on a lotus flower. The tashigomang is a complex teaching aid which the manip carries from place to place to instruct the then largely illiterate population the basic tenets of Buddhism. Wherever you happened to be in Bhutan in the town or countryside, you were constantly reminded of its Buddhist culture and tradition.

Before leaving Wangdi to continue on to Trongsa, I found a small corrugated iron shack tucked away in a corner of the square, serving as a cafe! One item on the menu that was guaranteed to be free of the flies in evidence, was 'momos'; -

delicious steamed parcels of chillied pork in an outer dumpling casing, served with very hot chilli sauce on the side. Taken with Indian style tea or 'chi', it was just the thing to keep me going until I reached my next overnight stop. The risk of an upset stomach as a result of eating momos is minimal even in a run down place like this, as the dish is kept continually steaming until served!

Suitably refreshed and fully fuelled, I set out on the next section of the journey along an unusually flat and exposed section of road high above the Dang Chu River for about 9 miles (15km) where a strong wind continually churned the dust into my face. Crossing to the other bank on another Bailey bridge; the road then climbed steadily onwards and upwards for no less than 28 miles (45km). It passed through tiny hamlets; beneath lofty sheer rock faces; and through forested areas festooned with bamboo. Up and up I travelled entering high altitude pine forest where every branch of every tree was draped with long streamers of lichen - a sure sign of how pure the atmosphere is at this altitude.

I planned to stay the night in the high glacial valley of Phobjikha, in an empty log cabin built some years before by a development agency that had pioneered potato growing there. Phobjikha 'valley' is at 10500 feet (3200m) above sea level. Shortly after passing through a village called Nobding, I had to leave the main road and climb for a short time up a steep un-surfaced dirt track to reach Phobjikha valley. This road was still under construction for almost all of its length, and the sunshine back in Wangdi had now given way to heavy continuous rain. The scooter skidded all over the place in deep slippery mud, and for much of the time I had to splay out my feet on either side like outriggers to keep upright.

Eventually I reached the top at a large white 'chorten' with characteristic red ochre band round the top; which marks the entrance into this high fertile valley, nestling amid forested mountains all around. From the chorten the road dropped gently down for some distance, until the tightly-knit village of Gangte came into view; dominated by Gangte Goemba a large monastery where young Buddhist monks undergo their initial training. Parking the scooter with my possessions on board at the side of the road knowing it would be perfectly safe until I returned; I walked up through the village to the entrance to the monastery. Here I was approached by two very young monks or **gaylongs**, one of whom surreptitiously produced some strange religious object from under his robe and tried his hardest to sell it to me! He was obviously disappointed at my lack of interest!

Below the monastery a broad flat and attractive valley stretches out with a stream running through the bottom and a few large houses dotted about. Willow trees flank the single track 'road' leading towards the valley's far end. This place has been of importance over many centuries and in recent years has gained even wider recognition for a very special reason. As the winter sets in, visitors arrive here each year from Tibet. Not by road but by air! Not by plane, but having winged their way from Tibet at an altitude of over 24,000 feet (7300m) over the Himalayan mountain range! They are Black-necked-cranes and this is one of very few places outside of their breeding habitat in Tibet where this rare bird can be seen. Their arrival in this valley each year is part of local folk lore, and is a significant event in the calendar. Paintings depicting these majestic birds are to be found throughout Bhutan and I was told that when the moon is full, pairs of cranes can be seen performing their graceful ritual courtship dance in the moonlight. When winter ends and the spring arrives these remarkable birds then leave Phobjikha, to return to their breeding grounds in Tibet; once more flying at the remarkable height of over 24,000 feet to clear the mountains!

The log cabin in which I spent the night was empty, dingy, and damp, and lacked any means of heating. Once again I was grateful for my four season's sleeping bag, as although it was summer and reasonably mild during the day, at this altitude it was decidedly chilly at night and just now was also decidedly dank. After a simple breakfast of a bar of chocolate, I made an early start to drive the next stage of my journey to the small but strategic town of Trongsa in central Bhutan, and was not sorry to leave my free but cheerless overnight accommodation.

Chapter 10

Bhutan by Motor Scooter - Central Bhutan

Thankful that the rain had stopped I slithered my way back down the unmade road and joined the main road once more. A further steady upward climb soon brought me to the top of the second mountain pass on Bhutan's lateral road, that of Pele la at 11,100 feet (3400m). A great vista of steaming forest stretched below and behind and to the north even the great Himalaya itself was completely obscured by a curtain of drifting cloud and vapour. The pass at Pele la marks the boundary between Eastern and Western Bhutan, so I was now leaving the district of Wangduephodang and entering that of Trongsa. The Black Mountains of Central Bhutan also wreathed in cloud, came partially into view in front of me after crossing the pass. Once more it was time to switch off the engine and silently coast downhill for mile after mile; the road leading down first through bare open mountainside yak pasture, then through pine forest, until it eventually flattened out and followed the course of yet another river.

Along the route I enjoyed intriguing cameos of Bhutanese village life and there were many fascinating sights to encourage me to stop and take photographs. A group of women compacting mud walls for a house under construction - worked in bare feet and were singing together as they trod the mud down between wooden shuttering. Another group of women were manually harvesting wheat by the curious method of pulling off the ears between two sticks, leaving the stalks standing to be cut down later or grazed by cattle.

I overtook a man carrying an enormous load of long bamboo poles on his back. He was striding purposefully along the road with his considerable burden with a smile on his face; head protected against sun and rain by a conical bamboo hat and a fine colourful homespun woollen cape over his shoulders. It never ceased to amaze me in Bhutan to see the multitude of different purposes to which bamboo was put! From hats to house construction and from drinking straws to pannier baskets! My many photos taken en route provide me with an invaluable visual diary as well as a vivid reminder of much of what I saw on my journey. Whenever I stopped in or near a village I was the source of polite curiosity. Westerners were still rarely seen outside of Thimphu - especially riding a motor scooter rather than travelling in a 4 x 4!

I took a welcome break on a river bank beneath a magnificent traditional cantilever bridge which gave access across the river to a village on the far side. It was ingeniously supported

127

on a series of timber bulks that projected from stone towers either side. Each tier of timber beams projected further out from both sides, until the final timbers carrying the wooden walkway itself, completed the spanning of the river. Along its length it was finished with a thatched roof and its decking fitted with a fine balustrade, making it safe for children, adults and animals to cross. All the timbers in these beautiful traditional wooden bridges are joined and pinned together using wooden dowels. Not one nail, screw, or bolt is used in their construction and I was told they are entirely built from memory; all of the knowledge and skill for their construction being passed down from one generation to the next simply by example and verbal instruction, as working drawings were still non-existent at that time.

Several miles further on by the side of the road, was a large and strange pyramidal structure of quite complex design, painted mostly white apart from a red ochre band around the top – telling me it was of religious significance. Near the top

of the pyramid large prominent eyes were painted. This I
found out later was Chendebji Chorten built in the 18th
century by a Tibetan Lama. Apparently it marks the western
limit of a 'chorten' path, followed by Buddhist missionaries
on pilgrimage.

For about 9 miles (15km) just beyond the Chorten, the road
was still under construction and was a continuous quagmire
of mud of indeterminate depth! This was one of very few
occasions when I saw heavy earth-moving equipment such as
bull dozers in Bhutan - obviously brought in from India
specifically for the road-building programme. My scooter
laboured manfully onward sometimes through muck nearly
a foot deep. When I was able to ride, I had to do so once again
with feet splayed out each side; with my trousers firmly
tucked into my socks, I furrowed a way through the mud.
Again and again I was forced to get off and manhandle the
scooter! With a rucksack on your back and treading in thick
mud it was no easy task! I must say it was a considerable relief
when, mud-splattered from head to foot, I reached the far end
of this section of unmade road, dirty but unscathed and found
myself on a proper metalled surface once more. Shortly
afterwards, very conveniently there was a waterfall cascading
onto the road, and I was able to wash down both the scooter
and myself.

Before Trongsa my destination for the night, came into view,
the road traversed several vertical rock faces where it had
been blasted out of a sheer cliff face. On the inside of the road
was a solid rock wall and at the outside edge, an
uninterrupted drop of several hundred feet. To the south the
land dropped away dramatically and from this lofty vantage
point, I had a breathtaking view through a tattered veil of

cloud of the Magde Chhu River, flowing thousands of feet below. This was not the place to meet a lorry without warning coming in the opposite direction! So I exercised extra special caution in rounding the many blind bends on this stretch of road. Finally, after rounding a bend on one of these hair-raising sections, Trongsa with its huge Dzong and cluster of imposing houses, suddenly came into view directly ahead of me - seemingly only a few hundred metres away. Its proximity proved to be an illusion!

Trongsa Town and Trongsa Dzong seen through monsoon cloud

Between where I was stood on the road and Trongsa, was a great steep-sided gorge many hundreds of feet deep. I could see a precipitous footpath leading down into the gorge and then climbing steeply up the other side to the Dzong after crossing the river on an old cantilever bridge. However, travelling on the road by scooter rather than by Shanks's pony required my driving for no less than a further 18 kilometres before I reached Trongsa.

I'd been recommended to stay at the 'Yangkhil' hotel; run by an educated Tibetan lady who was a member of a prominent and important ruling Tibetan family; who had fled Tibet along with her household following the Chinese invasion - eventually coming to settle in Trongsa. 'Ama' had now established a thriving hotel business with increasing trade from expatriate workers, looking for a clean bed and a hospitable place to stay. This was to be the first of many overnight stops here in years to come. Whenever I stayed here, Ama would remind me of this first visit when I'd arrived riding a motor scooter! It obviously made an impression.

On the ground floor of the 'hotel' was a room set out with chairs and tables in which you could stop for a drink or 'fooding' and from which a shop opened selling a simply amazing selection of goods; from wax candles to hand woven cloth, and from rice to rubber boots. The whole glassless shop front opened to the street, with heavy wooden shutters along its length hinging upward and fixed out of the way, to display her wares to anyone passing. Trongsa is at an altitude of 7000 feet (2120m) and experiences bitterly cold winters but those staying at Ama's guest house enjoy eating their meals in the warmth of a cosy kitchen at the back of the cafe - heated by a kitchen range manufactured by the 'Helvetas' bukhari workshop.

The best guest rooms were on the first floor and looked out directly over the bright orange roof of the enormous Dzong below. There was a shared washroom with a cold shower and 'drop' toilet. The latter is a feature of some of the more 'upmarket' houses, as most homes in Bhutan still had no indoor latrine of any kind. The 'drop' toilet gets its name because it is built on an upper storey and projects out from the side of the rest of the house to ensure that the 'waste products' drop vertically down a long chute into a cesspit at ground level. As the hotel Yangkhil is built on a steep mountainside there was a very considerable drop at the back of the building. Whenever I used the toilet I was reminded of a childhood experience at Carisbrook Castle in the Isle of Wight, where you judged the depth of the castle well by dropping a pebble and counting how long it took to splash at the bottom!

The massive Dzong standing just below the rest of Trongsa 'town' was built in 1648. It has been enlarged several times and is home to a large number of monks. The Dzong lies midway across Bhutan and once held a strategic position on the only ancient route connecting the eastern and western sectors of the country. This route passed through the Dzong itself, so its ruler or *'Penlop'* held a powerful controlling position. The first hereditary monarch Ugyen Wangchuck ruled the country from this ancient Dzong; and all of his successors before becoming King have held the post of Trongsa Penlop before their accession to the throne. Trongsa also marks the junction with the only road to go south in Central Bhutan, leading via the small town of Zhemgang, down to Gelegphu on the Indian border and following the Magde Chhu River for much of the way.

After a good meal and a sound night's rest in a clean and reasonably comfortable bed – a huge improvement on the damp log cabin of the night before; and having topped up with petrol at the Trongsa fuel station where fuel is pumped into a large cylindrical glass measure before being released into your tank; I deviated from my main route across country, to first head south to visit another hospital at a place called Yebilaptsa. My detour would take me about a day's drive in each direction.

Leaving Trongsa behind, the route south soon dropped downhill for many miles and again I coasted much of the way to conserve fuel. Spectacular vistas of the Magde Chhu River valley opened up, as the road followed the contours of the mountainside far above this major river several thousand feet below. Swirling tatters of cloud wreathed the landscape drifting over water-laden paddy fields which reflected the clouds in their mirror-like surfaces. My impression was of great pans of water forming a continuous series of contours mapping the steep valley side and dropping down like giant steps of glass toward the valley bottom. Not many miles from Trongsa, a spectacular waterfall tumbled down over an almost vertical rock face from hundreds of feet above; its spray cascading out directly over the road. It's difficult in such a landscape to have any true sense of scale or magnitude but a standard sized electricity pole carrying power from a small hydroelectric plant to a nearby village; was totally dwarfed by the immense height of the falls.

Once again I coasted silently, free-wheeling down through several small villages. As the road descended it threaded its way between paddy fields, twisting first one way and then back on itself via a succession of hairpin bends, time and time again; until eventually it levelled out on the bank of the fast flowing Magde Chhu River. This seemed a good place for me to stop and take a break. I sat on the river bank watching intrigued as a Brown Dipper dived a good ten feet down through the fast flowing water to feed on the river bottom. It was amazing to see this bird plunging so deeply as our native

British Dipper feeds only in shallow water. Though its Brown cousin lacked the distinctive white breast of the European Dipper, its bobbing motion when perched on a stone clearly identified it as a member of the same family. I could have lingered for longer, but not having travelled this route before and not knowing what else might face me before I reached Yebilaptsa; after just a short break it was prudent to press on.

For a few miles the road stayed close to the river and passed through one large village where untypically, some houses had 'enclosed cultivated garden' areas fenced around with bamboo; probably as a protection from deer and predators. Compared to the cold of Trongsa which I had only left behind a couple of hours before, it was a much kinder climate down here and there were many banana trees growing alongside the road. After several miles the road climbed again, up and out of the valley, entering natural mixed deciduous woodland and pine forest. In one place felled tree trunks were stacked high at the side of the road near to a saw pit. Two men laboured, manually sawing the trunks into planks ready for transportation. One had the unenviable task of being in the bottom of the pit pulling the crosscut downwards and so being enveloped in an intermittent shower of sawdust; whilst the man above was perched astride the log on planks and heaved the saw upwards after each cutting stroke. It was interesting that the wood being harvested was walnut – (a very expensive wood indeed in Europe), and had been brought from high above the road by 'sledging' it down steeply along an improvised chute cut through the forest. I gathered the timber was destined for use in a new conference hall being built in Thimphu.

Soon after this I found the road completely buried under a

recent landslip. Tons of rock and stone had been only partially cleared to allow vehicles to cross, but there was absolutely nothing to stop the unwary from plummeting from the outer edge down a thousand feet to the river below. Being on only two wheels, I was thankful it was not raining at the time and that the surface of the landslip was reasonably dry and I crossed over without mishap. The road and the Magde Chhu River now parted company; the river continued straight on through a narrow gorge, whilst the road turned sharply through ninety degrees and descended gently down following a tributary to cross over on a substantial concrete bridge; before beginning its climb upwards once again through another area of paddy fields by yet another series of hairpin bends, and in just a few miles elevated me a thousand feet or so, to bring me to the 'town' of Zhemgang.

Zhemgang is by far the largest settlement between Trongsa and the border town of Gelegphu. Yet apart from the Dzong and a primitive refuelling station where fuel was poured into my tank by hand using a metal funnel; it had neither 'shops' nor places for 'fooding and lodging' which would attract your trade unless you were really desperate! Even a place where I could buy a drink would have been welcome but there was obviously just not enough through traffic on this route to sustain any sort of business.

Leaving this rather forlorn place behind me the final 18 mile (30km) leg of my journey to Tintingbi was through almost unbroken sub-tropical forest in a steeply sided valley. Once again I could coast silently downhill on the narrow winding road which was fringed with overhanging fronds of bamboo. Here I was thrilled to have my first sight of the very rare and beautiful Golden Langur monkey when I came upon a troupe feeding in treetops almost level with the road. Apart from their small black faces, long golden hair covers the body down to the very tip of the tail. A female clutched a tiny youngster to her breast and even at this early stage in its life the baby was covered in golden hair!

The journey from Trongsa on this little used road had taken me about five hours and I had only met a couple of vehicles in the whole of that time. Just after reaching the small village of Tintingbi consisting of a few scattered houses and a saw mill; a dirt road, sign posted 'Yebilaptsa Hospital', branched off into the jungle. Climbing about four kilometres up an unmade track I finally reached the hospital complex on a small plateau surrounded by pine trees - in good time for afternoon tea!

The medical work at Yebilaptsa was being maintained by two English nurses, Joyce and Rosemary, working in partnership with staff from India, Nepal and Bhutan. Together they continued the battle to bring leprosy under control in this district and hopefully one day to effect its eradication. Due to the success of the leprosy work the number of new leprosy patients being admitted and treated at Yebilaptsa after six years' work was already steadily declining. Increasingly, the hospital was expanding its more general medical work - as this was the only hospital of any kind accessible from many of the tiny villages scattered on the mountainsides round about, in a sizable area of central Bhutan.

I think Joyce and Rosemary were rather surprised when I arrived by scooter so near to the expected onset of the monsoon. They warned me that the previous year they'd been cut off for six weeks by massive land slides which had severed the road in both directions! Despite the possibility of their being landed with me for rather longer than I'd planned, they made me most welcome. As they showed me round the hospital I never guessed for one second that a few years later I would be living here!

Mindful of the many miles I still had to go to complete my trip and that the weather was closing in, I only stayed at Yebi a day before driving back to Trongsa. Stopping briefly for something to eat, I then continued my journey east. Climbing up from Trongsa the road was well surfaced and I continued on to cover the further 42 miles (68 km) to Bumthang. There were no high mountain passes to negotiate and this was the easiest and shortest part of the whole journey. I had booked in once again at the Swiss Guest House so I knew I could look forward to a good meal and a comfortable night.

Fritz Mowher, who was in charge of the work of the Swiss agency Helvetas, had a stepson 'Jambay', who had come to train at The Royal Technical Institute the previous year. So I enjoyed a personally conducted tour by Fritz of the various projects the Swiss had been pioneering here since the 1960's. These included a vehicle repair workshop; a cheese-making project; an apple juice production and bottling plant; and a 'bukhari' manufacturing workshop. I stayed two nights at the guest house: to allow me time to explore the town and Dzong of Jakar; meet up with a fellow VSO teaching in the local school; and to find out what I could about the next and longest leg of my journey.

After this short break I felt ready for the long and most demanding drive over Thrimshingla, the highest of the mountain passes at 12300feet (3750m). Apart from a single village, this part of my route had no settlements along its complete length of 120 miles (193 km). The solitary compact village of Ura stands back off the road high up and in a very exposed position and there was no VSO teacher there that I might have stayed with. I also had to drive the 120 miles (193 km) to reach my next stop at Mongar, on only the 7 litres of fuel which my tank would hold; so my main concern was that the scooter might run out of petrol or fail me at such a high altitude. Once again my fears were unfounded as the Bajaj proved totally reliable never missing a stroke as it laboured steadily higher into gathering clouds; until I reached the highest point on my whole journey - which the sign at the top read as 12400 feet above sea level.

Though fortunately the really heavy monsoon rain had still not arrived, the top of the pass was enveloped in cloud and something of an anti-climax; for at this the highest point on my journey, I was denied the view of the Himalayas that I'd hoped for.

Chapter 11

Bhutan by Motor Scooter - Eastern Bhutan

About 25 miles (40 km) of this section was still a dirt track waiting for its surface layer to be applied; and large battered drums of tar lay along the route. At least the surface was still dry and I was able to traverse it easily enough, without having to negotiate a sea of mud. Once again it was very necessary to conserve fuel; turning off the ignition I coasted for many, many miles all the way down from the top of the pass until reaching the Kuru Chu River at the bottom; spanned by yet another beautiful traditional cantilever bridge.

I had made arrangements to stay at Mongar Leprosy Hospital with a British couple, John and Hilary Burslem. John was an ex Royal Marine surgeon and now the Medical Superintendent at Mongar. This hospital was the only one serving a large area and dealt with any and every medical case arising in the district; as well as with leprosy cases. As the monsoon rain was expected any day, after stopping just one night I decided to press on east without delay and possibly spend more time at Mongar on my return journey.

The next part of my route took me near Trashigang - the largest town in the north-east of Bhutan and then down toward the southern border with Assam. I planned to travel as far as a small cottage hospital at Risarboo; run by a Norwegian Mission with special responsibility for the leprosy work in this far eastern region of Bhutan. Throughout the day there were heavy showers - a portent that the monsoon rains were imminent. I was anxious not to be stranded in eastern

Bhutan, so on reaching the turn-off to Trashigang I continued without deviating, driving on south to Risarboo but resolved to visit Trashigang if possible on the return journey. A flight had been booked for my return to Britain and though it was still several weeks away, I was conscious that my only route back to Kharbandi might well be blocked by landslips at this time of year.

Risarboo hospital was built on a ridge overlooking a fertile valley and I reached there well before dark. Although we had never met, I was made most welcome by the doctor in charge. After a good night's rest and before I continued my journey south, the doctor asked if I would take a look at a small hydro-electric plant built to supply power to the hospital years before, but which had fallen into disrepair. Having electricity would make life at the hospital so much easier and she wanted to know if it might be possible at some time for the plant to be repaired and brought back on-line. The hydro-plant was situated far below the hospital in a narrow wooded river valley. As this was the time of year when snakes are a definite hazard I was accompanied by two Bhutanese staff members - one in front and one behind to look out for potential danger.

When we reached the valley bottom, I found it hard to believe that so many leeches could inhabit such a small area! There were leeches everywhere and as we walked an army of them issued from the ground and crawled over our boots. My trousers were tucked firmly into long socks to prevent anything going up the trouser legs but every few steps I had to stop and scrape leeches from my boots. It was a most unpleasant experience and I was rather glad when my inspection was over. Dripping with perspiration after the climb back up to the hospital, I stripped off and took a cold shower. It was then I discovered two leeches happily gorging themselves in between my toes! Amazingly, I can only think that they must have threaded themselves through an eyelet of my walking boots! They had to be given full marks for opportunism!

Next morning, I set off on the final day of my journey to reach the end of the road at Samdrup Jongkhar. This took me past a large army camp - the headquarters of the Indian Army Road Construction Corps. Outside the camp was a simple memorial to the several hundred road workers who had lost their lives during the construction of the tortuous mountain road across Bhutan which I had just traversed - mostly Nepali labourers but also some members of the Indian Army Corps, notably bulldozer drivers. Near to the camp was a golf course - only the second I knew of in Bhutan - the other being alongside Thimphu Dzong and patronised by the King and Ministers of State. This course obviously served the Indian Army and I was intrigued and rather amused to see one of the well-tended greens being carefully trimmed by a labourer - not with a lawn mower but on hands and knees equipped with an ordinary pair of domestic scissors!

Near the end of the afternoon I reached my final destination of Samdrup Jongkhar and could claim I had completed the journey west to east across Bhutan and be fairly confident that it was the first ever crossing on a motor scooter! I had driven 575 miles (930 km) from Phuentsholing, travelling on two rather small wheels, along a road with a less than perfect surface, with a rucksack on my back. By the time I arrived at Samdrup Jongkhar my shoulders seriously ached and even when I stopped travelling my whole body continued to vibrate and tingle in the most distracting manner!

In Samdrup Jongkhar an Irish Volunteer teacher was expecting me. Being an Indian border town like Phuentsholing, Samdrup Jongkhar boasts a variety of shops and Mary was able to survive here quite well. It was still a lonely place at this eastern extremity of Bhutan for a westerner to be based and Mary saw few visitors. She more than welcomed the chance to talk and catch up on news. After enjoying a welcome shower, a decent meal and Mary's company I felt somewhat more human.

The shortest direct route back to Phuentsholing is through Assam in India but as Assam is a sensitive military area and out of bounds to foreigners, I could not return that way. The thought of facing the return journey possibly battling the monsoon rain, was a daunting prospect. Following a good night's rest I was ready just, to try to cover as many miles as possible before the rains broke. I bade farewell to my charming Irish hostess and set off north toward Trashigang. I had only reached Risarboo when rain began to fall and I was persuaded (without too much resistance) to take a lift with a Norwegian doctor who happened to be travelling to Mongar via Trashigang. His Station Wagon could stow my scooter in the back and having driven the outward journey entirely by scooter I had no qualms about accepting his offer of a lift for part of this return leg.

To my delight we drove right into the centre of Trashigang, because my driver/doctor – who spoke Sharshopkha fluently - the eastern language of Bhutan, wished to pay a visit to a Bhutanese herbalist based here. Apparently he had been making regular visits to this man to find out as much as he could about the traditional herbal remedies that the herbalist dispensed. From Trashigang's main street we stepped directly into a fascinating room-come-shop the walls of which were shelved all round from top to bottom. These were filled completely with carefully labelled and stoppered jars, containing herbs, plants and potions. Bhutan has an ancient tradition of herbal medicine going back many centuries that the present government has encouraged to continue operating alongside the newly opened hospitals and clinics offering more western style medicine. My travelling companion sat and talked medicine with the herbalist for quite some time.

Who knows what effective drugs are still to be discovered from the plants found in the virgin forests of Bhutan? Another doctor who I knew who was a very experienced orthopaedic surgeon; worked at Mongar Hospital for two years following his retirement. He told me of one man that he had personally dealt with who had come to the hospital seeking treatment for a particular form of testicular cancer. The cancer was inoperable and so they were not able to offer any hope of cure. Several months later the doctor was amazed to see the same patient back at the hospital, not only very much alive but seemingly well and without any sign of cancer. The man said he had followed a traditional course of treatment from a herbalist and the cancer had disappeared!

When we reached Mongar a number of practical tasks awaited me. Working in a place like Bhutan where technical back-up services were almost non existent, meant that any person of a technical 'bent' might be asked to tackle all manner of practical problems! The only X-ray machine in the hospital was not producing the results that it should - could I investigate the possible causes? A brand new German Prosthesis machine for the manufacture of artificial limbs had been delivered but was not working. There were no circuit diagrams to help pinpoint where the fault might be - could I fix it? A covered walkway was required between two buildings - would I design one?

The variety of problems and the work involved in tackling them meant your knowhow and practical skills were used and stretched in a way that no job in the UK demanded. In Bhutan, a grasp of basic engineering principles, together with practical innovation, was what was required. When I left Mongar, I'd succeeded in getting the prosthesis machine to work after probing its circuits with an improvised test lamp made up from bits of wire, a light bulb and a battery; but I had only obtained very marginal improvement to the quality of pictures from the X-ray machine. I spent a morning exploring the 'town' of Mongar and found a beautiful example of traditional weaving to take home as a memento of my journey.

Continuing on I tried to travel whenever the rain eased and after two days had managed to reach Trongsa without too much trouble. Again I stayed overnight at the 'Yangkhil' hotel and enjoyed Ama's cooking. Next day however, to my consternation I found that a huge landslip had occurred just a mile out of Trongsa and had carried the road completely away. A gaping hole some twenty metres across was where the road had once been and it was obviously going to be a major task to rebuild it, so I had no choice but to stay on in Trongsa for several more nights. This was when I taught Ama to make potato chips and on my many subsequent visits to Ama's boarding house in years to come, chipped potatoes were always included on the menu! After driving to the site of the landslip on several successive days only to be turned back and told there was no possibility of getting across; on the fourth day an Indian army officer kindly arranged for my scooter to be portaged up the mountainside and over the top of the landslip, with me following along behind. My day of departure for Britain was drawing nearer and I had a plane to catch, so I was very thankful to be able to resume my journey. It was late in the morning before I had safely traversed the landslip and I still had the high mountain pass at Pele la to negotiate, followed by the long descent down the other side to Wangdi before I would reach a place to stay for the night.

On the long drive up toward the top of Pele la it began to rain in a continuous heavy downpour. The sky was overcast with low dark cloud and the light began to fail quite early in the afternoon. The monsoon proper had certainly arrived at last and with a vengeance! On crossing the pass, it was still a long way to Wangdi and essential to conserve fuel by coasting when possible; but in the driving rain I needed power even travelling downhill to give me stability on the now slippery road surface that was running in water like a river. Darkness fell and I was driving for the first time ever in the blackness by the rather feeble headlight beam of the scooter; which I discovered gave very limited vision in such appalling conditions. Suddenly, across the road in front of me the massive flank of a stationary bullock broadside-on loomed in the headlight out of the darkness. I don't know how I missed hitting it without running off the side of the road but the near miss was over and behind me before I even had time to blink the water out of my eyes! So on I travelled down the mountain road in the dark and the continuing deluge; soaked to the skin but thinking to myself that at least every mile was bringing me nearer to some kind of shelter for the night at Wangdi.

After many miles of descent near the bottom the road levels off and though it was totally dark, I knew roughly where I was. Suddenly without warning, the road beneath me was gone and I was ploughing through a sea of mud in the darkness. I had no idea what was happening and simply tried to keep my cool and maintain the scooter's forward momentum and keep roughly on a level across the expanse of sludge which stretched way beyond the limit of my feeble headlight - merging into the blackness. I slithered and slid forwards in fits and starts managing to make progress little by little and somehow keeping the scooter from sliding sideways and downwards. It was with tremendous relief that after about a hundred metres and what seemed like an eternity I regained the road as suddenly as I had lost it. It was only long after the event, that I learned that a huge landslip had completely buried the road at this point under a sea of mud; and that debris had cascaded down over the road and on into the forest below. Looking back on my experience I could so easily have slid over the edge and down into the void and darkness, with very little chance of anyone ever finding me even if I survived.

A few miles further and the road reached the bottom of an overhead cable ropeway, built by the Swiss in the 1970's to carry timber and people to several villages high above. I remembered being told that at this lower end there was a house where at one time you could find shelter. As the deluge showed no sign of abating and visibility was still only a few yards, I decided to avoid any further possible mishaps and would try to gain access and spend the night here. A weak glimmer of light shone from the house through the watery blackness and in response to my knocking the door was opened by a rather startled old man who beckoned me in out of the downpour. With typical spontaneous Bhutanese hospitality, in no time I was warming up before a fire while he cooked rice and chilli for our supper. I retired for the night on the floor in a somewhat damp sleeping bag absolutely worn out. After a fitful night, I awoke early next morning to find the old man who did not speak one word of English, cooking a breakfast for us of egg together with the left over rice from the night before.

Mercifully the rain had stopped and after expressing my thanks to the kindly and hospitable old man, I was able to continue on my way to Wangdi. On reaching the main square I made straight for the small corrugated iron café for a plate of 'momos' to keep me going for the rest of the day. Part way through my meal the then Coordinator of the Leprosy Mission in Bhutan walked in. He by chance was also in Wangdi and was interested to hear details of my journey and particularly of the visits to the various hospitals. This led us to a general discussion about the ongoing maintenance of the hospitals and the need for a peripatetic technical person to oversee the upkeep of both buildings and equipment. He asked if I would be interested in such a post but at the time my now-imminent return to Britain was uppermost in my thoughts. It's very possible however, that this chance meeting had a bearing on my eventual return to work in Bhutan in years to come, this time for the Leprosy Mission.

With a good helping of momos inside me I set off to cross the last mountain pass of Dochu la in time to reach Gidakom before nightfall. As I began to climb once more out of the Wangdi valley so the rain began again and became progressively heavier. The huge rhododendron bushes flanking the sides of the road glistened and ran with water. Low cloud cloaked the top of the pass and I drove over without stopping, coasting as much as was safely possible down the other side toward the Thimphu valley. I must admit it was a welcome relief to reach the comfort of Steen and Lisbeth Anderson's guestroom at Gidakom, and following two very wet days and a damp night, to at last dry out and enjoy a good meal with friends and the luxury of a nights sleep in a comfortable bed. With my enforced delay in Trongsa due to the land slip, time was now getting short to pack up and be ready for my departure for Britain and the next day I continued south reaching Kharbandi well before nightfall.

My shoulders ached and my arms continued to experience tingling sensations for weeks afterwards - but I had made it and had greatly enjoyed seeing as much as I had of this remarkable country, before leaving for home! I had fulfilled my ambition to complete a 'grand tour' of Bhutan; I had enjoyed the company and hospitality of like-minded people at the various hospitals and other overnight stops; and it had been instructive to see and learn at first hand the development and medical work going on across Bhutan. The whole experience had been rewarding - most of the time - and a great way to bring to a close my three years in this fascinating country before no doubt with its rapid emergence into the twentieth century it would change for ever.

My three years with VSO were up! I'd been asked to consider another teaching post over in the east at the 'Polytechnic'; but I felt it time to pick up the threads of my life again and I was looking forward enormously to seeing family and friends

148

after another year's absence. I needed to find a job; accommodation, and to readjust to living once more in the society I'd left behind three years ago; that '**Other World** ' so different in so many respects to this Himalayan Kingdom called Bhutan that had been my home. I wondered how on earth I would settle in Britain into a routine teaching post after such an experience. I was not yet aware of the degree to which the past three years had changed my outlook and how that experience would influence my life again in the near future.

It was with very mixed feelings that a week later plus two days sat at Paro airport waiting for a window in the weather, through which the plane could land and take off safely; I finally left for home not knowing whether I would ever return to re-visit my good friends and colleagues who I was now leaving behind in this other world.

Chapter 12

TWO for the Price of One + Jock!

I met my wife-to-be during my home leave in 1986 before returning to teach for a third year at Kharbandi, and we corresponded with each another for the twelve months I was away again in Bhutan. After I'd returned home - I thought for good, we were married in November 1987. Three years of frugal living was still fresh in my consciousness; Dot on the other hand had never lived outside of Britain and found it difficult at times to appreciate my very different point of view - so our first months of married life together was an interesting time of adjustment for us.

Eighteen months later the Leprosy Mission asked me to consider working as the 'Project Manager' for what they termed a 'Hospital Expansion Project' at the remote hospital at Yebilaptsa - which of course I'd visited during my 'grand tour.' To help us make our minds up, we made a six week exploratory visit to Yebilaptsa in April 1989. At the end of that visit we both reached the same conclusion independently of one another; that the situation both at home and in Bhutan was **not** right to allow us to relocate there at that time.

Two years later we were again approached. Time was running out for The Leprosy Mission. If a start on the Yebilaptsa 'Hospital Expansion' Project was not made that year, the funding pledged by the German government would be withdrawn. Our personal circumstances had changed by this time and we now felt we should go. So after a round of formal interviews and having made a joint will; we packed up house and home, put our belongings into storage, had our medicals and all the vaccinations you can think of; and in September 1991 left to work in Bhutan for the next three years.

TLM (The Leprosy Mission) thought it best that we stay at Gidakom while I was tackling the preparatory work needed before actual construction at Yebilaptsa could begin. We were accommodated in the Gidakom 'guest' bungalow where I'd often stayed before. The bungalow was wood framed with a tin roof and with bare wooden floors and was basic but adequate. It had a lounge with wood stove; a tiny kitchen, bathroom and two bedrooms - one of which I used as an office. We had the luxury of electric light and hot water from an electric water heater because Gidakom was connected to an electricity supply from the very first hydroelectric plant in Bhutan. It was built to supply Thimphu but as it happened to be just down the valley from Gidakom, the hospital also benefited. Compared to our accommodation at Yebilaptsa, Gidakom was definitely five stars!

Our arrival was hardly auspicious. Dorothy woke me in the middle of our first night feeling very unwell and seconds later passed out cold on the floor. She was ill for several days with vomiting and diarrhoea and we suspected the problem was the ice cubes added to her orange juice on the flight from Delhi. We knew the precautions one has to take with food and drink on the Indian sub-continent; that you should only drink bottled juice or water; you should not eat salad unless it's been washed in purified water; and not to add ice cubes to your drink as they may be made of impure water! But who thinks of such things when cruising in a comfortable British Aerospace 146 'whispering jet' at 28000 feet (8200m) over the Himalayas - looking to the top of Mount Everest across the most incredible vista of the highest mountain range in the world?

In addition to her nausea Dot was not able to sleep due to a racing heart - caused by sudden relocation from sea level in Kent to about 8000 feet (2400m) at Gidakom. The air is noticeably thinner at this altitude - another way of saying it contains less oxygen. This can cause nausea, splitting headaches and shortness of breath - especially when exerting oneself in any way. Until the body acclimatises to the change, the heart has to work harder to supply the vital organs, particularly the brain, with the amount of oxygen they need. When you've lived continually at altitude for about a month, amazingly the body 'acclimatises' and the number of red blood corpuscles is naturally increased enabling your blood to absorb oxygen more efficiently and so compensate for the decreased level of oxygen in the air. My daughter Alison had already been working at Gidakom in charge of the nursing team for three years by the time Dot and I arrived, and had fully adjusted to the very different conditions and the altitude. She provided us with meals to begin with and was able to help Dot through the sickness and begin adjusting to her new life.

Gidakom hospital was now under the supervision of Dr Steen Andersen; and the hospitality I had enjoyed in years past from the Riedel's, was continued by Steen's wife Lisbeth who was a homely individual and a good cook, with the invaluable skill to conjure up imaginative and appetising meals out of the simplest ingredients. The Andersen's invited us to meals - especially during the first few weeks when Dot was making huge adjustments in going to Bhutan to live.

It was a real culture shock, moving from Britain where she'd lived all her life to come to this remote place with none of the modern conveniences we take for granted in the 'West'. Apart from the electric water heater there were no mod-cons. No washing machine, no vacuum cleaner, no food mixer, no central heating, no refrigerator and no freezer. Mind you, it was so cold at Gidakom especially in winter you could manage without a refrigerator; and there was nothing you could purchase to store in a freezer anyway! We were blessed with a western style pedestal flush toilet but even then it proved necessary for me to clear the sewage system periodically when it got blocked! Domestic life had certainly returned to basics in more ways than one.

There was no popping down to the supermarket or corner store when Dot ran out of something. At a tiny booth outside the hospital entrance you could buy eggs, soap, rice and matches - but very little else. This lack of a local store which Dot had taken so much for granted, demanded a complete change in her thinking about shopping and the planning of meals. Once a week on a Saturday, the hospital vehicle made the 60 kilometre round shopping trip to Thimphu, so you could buy vegetables in its large open market and any other groceries you required from the various shops in Thimphu's main street. However, the limited seats available on the hospital vehicle meant that not everyone could go shopping every week; so staff had to take it in turns to shop on a rota basis. If it was not your turn and you needed groceries, you gave a list to the driver and he would shop for you.

At the end of the first week Dot didn't feel much like journeying to Thimphu but we had to think about stocking up with food for the following week just the same - so she made out a list for the driver. When her order was delivered our tiny kitchen looked like a harvest festival with vegetables filling the place. It was then we realised there had been some confusion over 'units'. What Dot had ordered in English pounds the driver had purchased in kilograms so she'd ended up with more than double what she wanted! Even this remote Kingdom had adopted kilos; whereas in Britain we were still stubbornly hanging on to our imperial pound! It took us quite a time to use a quarter of a kilogramme of garlic!

Dot's days were taken up with baking bread without a bread maker; washing clothes without a washing machine; the essential boiling, filtering and then bottling of every drop of water required for drinking and cooking; cleaning out the wood stove and getting in a supply of logs; as well as devising a hundred and one ways of using tinned tuna fish! We both had to learn to cut one another's hair as there was no professional hairdresser nearer than the Indian border - six hours drive away. Lisbeth did it for us to begin with until we plucked up the courage to take on the task ourselves. This took a lot of faith and tolerance on Dot's part, as she has naturally curly hair that takes a degree of skill to cut well! I was quite happy with a traditional short back and sides!

Of course there was no television, no CD player, no computer and no library and our evenings took on a different routine altogether; usually huddled close to the one source of heating - a primitive log stove. Arriving in September we were soon enduring the bitterly cold Bhutanese winter experienced at these high altitudes. Most days the sun shone out of a clear sky and though the ground was frozen it would be pleasantly warm outside. But as the hospital is in the bottom of a deep, steeply sided valley, at about four in the afternoon as soon as the sun disappeared below the rim of the surrounding mountain tops, the temperature plummeted to way below zero.

The only means of heating the bungalow was a primitive wood stove or *'bukhari'* in the middle of the lounge. It had a 'door' in the front through which you lit it and fed it with logs, and a stove pipe coming out the top which disappeared through a hole in the ceiling - meant to carry away the smoke! The stove had a mind of its own and after what could be an age to get it lit, depending on the strength and direction of any wind outside and whether or not the wood was properly dry; it either provided heat as intended and discharged the smoke up the chimney, or it was just as likely to send the smoke in clouds into the room while the heat dissipated up the chimney! We would stoke up the bukhari and huddle close to it for warmth until quite early in the evening we were convinced we'd be better off in bed! There was no heating in the bedroom and so we would retire buried under a mound of bedclothes plus padded quilt and anything else we could find heaped on top - and still we'd feel cold. When the outside temperature was exceptionally low (which was often) we slept dressed in our thermal vests and long-johns and at such times longed for our eventual move to the **sub-tropical** conditions at Yebilaptsa, where frost is unknown!

Without any encouragement on our part we were befriended by a dog - or rather an attractive black and tan short haired bitch which would regularly appear at our door for any scrap of food going. So many dogs roam the towns and villages in Bhutan not belonging to anyone in particular - we had no idea where this friendly bitch came from. She would be found curled up in a tight ball outside the bungalow in the morning her dark coat covered in a thick layer of frost! Coming from a nation of animal lovers we were disturbed at the thought of her suffering out in the cold, so we tried to coax her inside to warm up. Eventually she would creep just inside the door but only for ten minutes and then she'd whine to go out again.

After several months our friendly bitch turned up with a lovely puppy in tow; which we imagined was hers though we'd not noticed she was pregnant. The puppy proved to be much more adaptable than his mother and soon seemed as much at home inside the bungalow as out! We named him 'Jock' (Dot being a Scot) and adopted him as our house dog and Jock proved to be quite a character. He never had to be housetrained and from the start barked to be let out if he needed to toilet. Unlike his mother Jock was perfectly content to stay in all night and though he proved to be a good house dog, mercifully he seldom joined in when the dogs outside began howling. Dogs in Bhutan create an awful din at night, as when one dog starts barking all the others will join in, until your slumber is shattered by a cacophony of barking and yapping from near and far, and you are driven in desperation to try and block out the noise buried completely under the bedclothes! First thing each morning Jock would push open the bedroom door, walk to the side of our bed and engage us in quite an animated conversation. He would tilt his head first to one side and then to the other accompanied by friendly grunts and growls, until one of us got up and let him out. When we relocated to Yebilaptsa Jock came with us and stayed there throughout the rest of our time in Bhutan. More about Jock later!

The advantage for me of living at Gidakom was that Thimphu was only an hour's drive away; rather than the two days' drive when we relocated to Yebilaptsa. There was a multitude of problems to be addressed and a lot of vital Project detail still to be sorted. In the absence of a reliable telephone service I needed to make numerous visits to offices in Thimphu as well as down in Phuentsholing before any construction work could begin at Yebilaptsa.

I began design work almost immediately after appraising what vital preparations still needed to be done; producing the numerous detailed drawings that were needed on a small A2 Drawing Unit. The rather unusual conditions under which I was working gave rise to problems no-one could or would have foreseen. The ink cartridge pens used in most modern drawing offices in preference to a pencil, proved to be extremely temperamental - when required to work in the freezing cold and at 8000 feet above sea level! The ink didn't want to flow, the nibs clogged up, and when you finally got a pen to work, the ink just would not dry! Even the following day my drawings would still smudge, making a real mess of the work of the previous day!

One 'perk' of being the Project Manager was in having a 4 x 4 vehicle provided - as the job required a great deal of travelling. Soon after our arrival I was asked what vehicle I would like ordered so that it could be imported. The TLM Coordinator had recently taken delivery of a new Suzuki Trooper from Japan and as this model was also suitable for my needs and the paper work was still on file; thinking it would expedite matters I requested the same vehicle and model be ordered for the Project. This logic proved to be a mistake and for many months I was stuck with a rather old and well-used Toyota Land Cruiser owned by TLM but which had certainly 'seen better days' and long since been replaced for medical work, by a new vehicle.

On several occasions driving the old Toyota I dearly wished I'd taken time to attend a car maintenance course. The first happened between Gidakom and Yebilaptsa when in the middle of nowhere the vehicle ground to a halt in a cloud of black smoke. With no AA or RAC to call upon there was no other course of action but to investigate the cause of the breakdown myself. Having experienced the clogged fuel filter during Alison's visit I guessed this might be at the root of the problem on this occasion. Removing the filter, sure enough I found it clogged up with sludge. I'd just got it back in place after a thorough cleaning and was ready to test the engine when a vehicle drew up and two young men got out grinning widely. 'It looks as if two students from Kharbandi have arrived', Dot commented. Sure enough two motor mechanics from five years past had miraculously appeared like genies from a lamp in the middle of nowhere! They insisted on double checking the system for a second time before letting us go on our way!

The circumstances surrounding our second breakdown were much more frightening and could easily have resulted in a serious accident. We were driving back to Gidakom from Phuentsholing after a Project meeting to discuss a contract. About half way home on a typically tortuous section of mountain road - without warning I found there was no response from the brake pedal! I was going downhill at the time and only about fifty metres in front of me was a tight, right angled bend with a solid rock face facing me on the bend. Mercifully I was not travelling very fast, as the only thing I could do to slow the vehicle, was to crunch down through the gears. There was no way I could call for help and we were still many miles from Gidakom; so rather than remain in the middle of nowhere until help *might* eventually arrive, our only other option was to crawl along in low gear for the rest of the journey. We arrived back at Gidakom late that night but thankfully still in one piece. I was more than relieved, when after about ten months of waiting and several vehicle problems later, the new Project vehicle finally arrived.

When I was appointed Project Manager I understood my job would involve keeping accounts; dealing with correspondence; liaising with contractors, suppliers and the local Dzongda; monitoring quality and progress; and making quarterly reports to the German donor. I understood from what TLM had told me that the hospital plans were complete and the Project cost calculated; so once a suitable contractor was found my main task would be to oversee construction and generally facilitate the completion of the Project. When we arrived I found the situation very different to what I expected. Before there was any possibility of the Project being offered for tender and the preferred contractor/s selected, a considerable number of important tasks still remained to be tackled.

Over the twenty years TLM had been working in Bhutan, their leprosy hospitals at Gidakom, Mongar, Lhuntshi and Yebilaptsa had grown piecemeal in response to medical need and as funding became available. In those early days there were no architects or civil engineers available, nor could they call for help on a telephone. So in these pioneering days, buildings were designed in a fairly elementary way by resourceful TLM doctors and nurses, using their initiative and local labour.

The Yebilaptsa Project on the other hand, would be by far the biggest single building project that TLM had undertaken in Bhutan. The Project title of 'Hospital Expansion' - though true in one sense was something of a misnomer. It was true that a small hospital at 'Yebilaptsa' was already established and the Project would certainly represent an 'expansion' of its facilities. **But** as far as the hospital *buildings* were concerned this Project would provide a new, considerably bigger, and properly designed hospital. It would now serve as a **General Hospital** that could also treat the occasional leprosy patient; rather than continue as a specialised leprosy hospital.

Preparatory work on the hospital's design had been completed two years before in 1989 by a qualified Civil Architect, Rob Fielding. I knew Rob because he had also been employed through VSO - for designing new primary schools in Bhutan; at the same time as I was teaching at Kharbandi. Rob had produced a proposed layout for the new Yebi hospital and identified where it could be located on the wooded hillside which Yebilaptsa occupies. After carrying out a preliminary site survey, Rob had also produced elevations of the new buildings at their various levels on the site.

Rob's underlying concept was for the appearance of the hospital to be in keeping with Bhutan's traditional architecture. The hospital entrance should resemble the entrance to a Dzong as this was the only other public building that most villagers would know. The hospital doors and windows should be of the distinctive Bhutanese style. The various buildings should be grouped around several open courtyards reminiscent of the courtyards in a Dzong. This layout would provide good natural lighting and maximise the air flow needed to keep building's as cool as possible in this sub-tropical region. Rob's whole design aimed to ensure that people arriving at the hospital from outlying districts would feel at home and familiar with the appearance of the building.

PERSPECTIVE
OPERATING THEATRE COURTYARD

Architect Rob Fielding's design concept for a 'people friendly' hospital

Another integral part of Rob's design was for every building to have a wide covered veranda which would link all the separate buildings together. As well as providing shade this would permit the easy movement of staff and patients around the hospital without exposure to torrential rain in the monsoon. In addition to the open courtyards there would also be a number of covered public areas; where recuperating patients and their relatives could sit under the shelter of a roof - protected from direct sun and from rain. Being built on a sloping site, it would prove necessary to link together the four different levels within the hospital with a system of ramps, enabling staff to transport patients easily to any part of the hospital.

There were no Building Control Officers in Bhutan to ensure that plans were followed correctly; that a building was constructed properly without 'cutting corners'; and to prevent cheating on the materials used etc. so that would be a part of my job as Project Manager. The basic structural design and specification needed to be decided upon - stipulating details such as the thickness and mix of concrete and the size and design of steel reinforcing. Materials had to be sourced. A fully detailed and dimensioned drawing for each individual building was needed. The building costs had to be recalculated in the light of inflation. A fair method for paying the contractors for work done had to be devised that would also keep the work moving forward. A major Project like Yebi Hospital could be exploited and over-run its budget if it was not properly supervised; and a legally binding contract between TLM and the contractor/s was needed.

So there was a lot more work and planning required before the Project could literally be 'got off the ground', and in a comparatively short time to meet the German time limit for the funding. Another important decision to be made was whether to offer the Project for tender as a whole, or in stages. After some thought, I decided to sub-divide the contract into three. This was partly because of the amount of detailing work still needed; partly because of the need to begin construction as soon as possible; and last but not least, so that each completed Phase could be handed over for immediate hospital use and the medical staff would gain the extra facilities it needed as soon as was possible.

Near the end of five frantic months working on these preliminaries, it was a landmark day when I was able to place a formal **'Notice of Tender'** in the national newspaper 'The Kuensel'. Four tenders were received by the deadline set and I had the task of deciding who should be offered the work. The major contract was awarded to **'Yarkey Construction'** - an established firm of reasonable size and repute. I never regretted my decision and they proved to be a competent and efficient company, with whom I enjoyed a good working relationship free of major disputes. At last the construction work could be scheduled to begin at Yebilaptsa from May 1992.

The Royal Government had stipulated that a suitably qualified Bhutanese should be appointed as my 'Counterpart' to work alongside me and so gain experience that could then benefit other projects. One of my last tasks before moving to Yebi was to appoint this 'Counterpart'. Again I advertised in the 'Kuensel' and received nine applications and after interviewing all nine I chose Deepak Pradhan; a young man in his mid twenties who had done well in the Bhutanese school system and gone on to study Civil Engineering before joining the Roads Department of the Government. This choice was approved by Government early in 1992 without objection. His contract with TLM would continue until the Project was finished.

It made a huge difference for me to receive from Dot all the support and encouragement I needed in the work I was doing. When I experienced setbacks and difficulties as I did, Dot was the one who kept me focussed and who I could always rely on for support to bring me out on the other side. Nor did I have to think about the shopping, cooking, cleaning, washing of clothes, etc., as I had done during my years teaching at Kharbandi. In taking on all of the domestic chores Dot made her own substantial contribution to the success of the Project. Without her willing and unstinting support, Yebilaptsa Hospital would certainly not have been completed so successfully or as speedily.

By the time we were ready to transfer our base to the even more remote location at Yebilaptsa; Dot had settled down and adjusted well to her new way of life. She had had to make enormous adjustments to living in this strange land; to tolerate the very basic living conditions; and endure the sometimes harsh climate. She was also bereft and cut off from her many friends back home as well as her 'bairns'; not to mention still being in the early years of our married life together after being a widow for five years! Now we were to uproot once more and move to yet another situation and climate at Yebilaptsa!

The buildings that comprised Yebilaptsa hospital

We'd had to decide where we would live at Yebi so that it could be made ready and our choice was a staff bungalow which at one time had been occupied by the English nurse Mollie Clarke who had founded the hospital. It was at the far end of a line of staff bungalows, and a definite plus in its favour was the western style toilet! By knocking down a dividing wall the bungalow was to be enlarged to accommodate us and provide me with an office from which I would manage the Project. My office also doubled as our guest bedroom. At last in April 1992 all the preparations were complete. We could move base to Yebi, and we were more than happy at the prospect of getting the actual building work under way at last; in the knowledge that this Project should make a significant difference to the welfare of many thousands of people in this central region of Bhutan.

Measured on the map, Thimphu and Yebilaptsa are only 70 miles (110km) apart in a straight line; yet the drive by road was over 250 miles (400km)! Travelling at an average maximum speed of 20 – 25 miles/hour (32 – 40 km/hour), it was a long and demanding journey over two days with an overnight stop at Trongsa. Heading south from Trongsa on the Gelegphu road and shortly after passing through the small 'town' of Zhemgang located high on a mountain ridge, you have your first glimpse of Yebilaptsa hospital - a small cluster of buildings perched up above the Mangde Chhu river valley in a forest clearing. Not many kilometres beyond Zhemgang we reached the small village of Tintinbi, and on its far edge a sign pointed up a rough track to 'Yebilaptsa Hospital' which wound its way about four kilometres through jungle to a plateau set amid pine trees. At last we'd reached Yebilaptsa where we would be living for the next two years.

Dot and Jock on our way to Yebilaptsa with all but the kitchen sink!

Chapter 13

Survival in the Back of Beyond

In moving base to Yebilaptsa our first concern was how Jock would travel as he had never left Gidakom before nor ridden in a vehicle. Most of the journey he was an exemplary passenger and even slept in the vehicle at the overnight stop without a problem - not even a puddle on the floor! But he nearly didn't make it to his new home! The final part of our journey from Zhemgang was through sub-tropical forest and as we rounded a bend, a whole troupe of Golden Langur monkeys leapt across in front of us! Jock, who was sat between us up front, instantly jumped across Dot and was half out of the open window in hot pursuit before she managed to restrain him! Had she failed, Jock may well have been lost forever in the jungle of Bhutan. We grew to love Jock dearly, but had he disappeared into the jungle life would have been less trouble and much duller for all those at Yebilaptsa!

Yarkey Construction had set up their labour camp in readiness. They had installed a water supply to the camp; dug latrines; as well as erect a site office and a secure store. The largely Indian labour force didn't complain about conditions because they'd guaranteed employment for the next two years at an equivalent rate of 60p a day; which was twice what they could earn in India - were they able to find work there. By comparison we were super rich, being paid the same as everyone else working overseas for the Leprosy Mission, including their nurses and doctors - about £ 3000 a year plus free accommodation!

Our free accommodation was a very basic bungalow, but it

represented a reasonable standard of housing for Bhutan. The TLM carpenter from Assam Praffula Mandal had worked hard making many improvements before we arrived. Installing mesh shutters over the window and door openings to keep out the mosquitoes; fitting a basic 'bukhari' wood stove in what would be our living room; equipping the 'kitchen' with a concrete work top and a small cockroach proof food cupboard; as well as making our furniture such as a table for us to eat on, chairs for us to sit on, a wardrobe and a double bed to sleep in! Mandal was to prove invaluable to me in so many ways on the Project; and over the next two years to become a good friend to us both and Jock as well!

Our new home had a bare concrete floor; plaster on bamboo wattle walls; a galvanised tin roof and a general lack of what you might regard as 'mod cons'. However, we did have the luxuries of water on tap in the kitchen; a flush toilet; and a *de luxe, crème de la crème* 'bucket shower' in the 'washroom'. Our 'bucket shower' was the height of sophistication! It consisted of the largest galvanised metal bucket I could purchase, with a rose and tap plumbed in the bottom; plus a rope and double pulley system to haul it up into a space in the ceiling. Having made sure that your soap, etc. was all to the ready, we would fill it with hot water from a pan heated on the bukhari and then hoist it into the ceiling. You could enjoy a decent shower, wash your hair and still luxuriate for half a minute under an ample spray of warm water, before it ran out. The only one who disliked the shower was Jock. He fought (almost tooth and nail) to avoid getting wet but after a struggle would succumb to the inevitable and allow me to wash him. Needless to say I got as wet as Jock did in the process and as soon as his shower was over and before I could get him outside - he would violently shake the water off his coat - all over me.

Our bungalow was at the end of a line of similar staff bungalows, stretched out along the rim of the mountain plateaux which the hospital complex occupies. We looked down a steep jungle clad hillside to the river far below and being on the outer rim of the ridge benefited from any slight breeze created by the thermals rising up the mountainside. Though our new home was basic it had an outlook that no money could buy – looking down the valley between interlocking fingers of the mountains into the distance!

When we first arrived our only electricity was supplied from two old and basic solar panels which charged up two 12v batteries. Yebi enjoyed plentiful sunshine most of the year so the solar panels worked fine. Praffula Mandal knew absolutely nothing about electricity so reconfiguring the DC wiring system fell to my lot. One battery provided power for a small fluorescent tube giving just sufficient light to knit, read or play Scrabble by, for about two hours. As we tended to rise early with the dawn by the time the electricity gave out we were exhausted anyhow and ready for bed. We grew to enjoy this natural daily cycle of life governed largely by the sun.

A solar refrigerator was powered by the second 12v battery. This was a fantastic facility as the weather became so hot during the summer. The DC fridge served us well until my counterpart Deepak stayed in the bungalow during our home leave in the summer of 1992! By this time a hydroelectric plant in the valley nearby had been completed and mains electricity had been installed in the staff bungalows. Deepak demonstrated his abysmal knowledge of electricity when he connected our DC refrigerator to the new AC mains and literally 'blew it' – sadly the solar fridge never worked again! We eventually managed to obtain a replacement AC refrigerator from Phunsholing - delivered after a two-day journey in the back of an open lorry!

The spare bedroom doubled as my office where I spent a considerable amount of time. Beside the single bed – strictly for visitors - the only other furniture was a table and chair in front of the window and a very ancient typewriter. I was responsible for all the correspondence and for writing the quarterly progress reports for the donors but because I am somewhat heavy handed on a keyboard, the old typewriter punched a hole in the page every time I typed 'o'! I didn't have time to worry about what staff in the London headquarters of TLM made of these 'holy' reports, but 'O' how I could have done with a lap top computer!

What my office lacked in equipment it more than made up for in outlook facing down the valley. It was an inspirational view to look out upon, as each day dawned and as the rising sun gradually filled the valley with colour and heralded in another day. During monsoon the rain came down in a solid sheet - hammering on the galvanised iron roof and making it difficult to think let alone hold a conversation. But when the rain ceased and the sun broke through, a veil of mist and vapour lifted by the heat of the sun, gradually revealed more and more of the valley. Clouds actually drifted *through* our bungalow - entering in by the open meshed windows on one side and passing out through the open meshed doors on the other.

Much of the year we enjoyed the wonderful panoramic view

and sometimes as we sat having lunch we would watch a White Tailed Fish Eagle soaring by level with our window! A concrete 'patio' at the back of the bungalow extended to the very edge of the mountainside where sometimes we could sit outside and enjoy the view - provided the mosquitoes and sand flies were not in a biting mood. We found the mosquitoes preferred me, whereas sand flies preferred Dot, who constantly suffered a multitude of bites around her ankles. Thankfully, the mosquitoes up here did not carry malaria, yet those just the short distance away in the valley did; so it was still necessary for us to take anti-malarial tablets.

Our isolated and basic lifestyle did have its compensations. Bhutan is a paradise for anyone interested in wildlife. One day Dot and I were walking on a forest path near the hospital when we heard a very loud whooshing noise bearing down on us. A Giant Hornbill - easily recognised by its distinctive black and white plumage and striped tail as well as by its massive curved yellow bill, flew low overhead with its huge wings thrashing the air. This species of Hornbill is common throughout the south of Bhutan and we saw them again many times but never at such close quarters. On another occasion we saw no less than six of a much rarer bird, the Rufous-necked Hornbill, feeding in trees bordering the road. This species was last recorded in nearby Nepal where it was once common, more than 150 years ago in the 1840's. This distinctive bird has unmistakable and spectacular colouring - with a bright crimson breast, large electric blue eye patches, and a striped bill. Bhutan has managed to preserve most of its forest and for that reason still retains the exotic birds and beasts that have been found here for hundreds if not thousands of years.

Bhutan has such a huge variety of different butterflies and

moths I doubt they have all yet been fully listed! At Yebi there were tropical butterflies the size of a man's hand. Some butterflies were so abundant that as you drove along they would rise up in hundreds from a mineral rich patch of damp earth at the side of the road. We both enjoyed seeing the abundant bird and animal life around us.

One form of wildlife Dot abhors is snakes and she vowed that if she saw one it would herald her immediate return home! Of course there were many in the jungle and occasionally they came onto the building site. I saw them but Dorothy didn't, apart from one large specimen that we drove over on the road not far from Yebi in a fully laden Land Cruiser. The snake hardly paused on its way into the jungle, seemingly none the worse for being run over apart from a distinctly flattened section in its middle!

We had a small open garden area around the bungalow, in which grew the biggest poinsettia you can imagine - the size of a bush, and there were orange and banana trees. During the hotter months a large brightly coloured lizard with a fine red crest would scuttle up Dot's clothes pole and bask there in the heat of the sun. One day we discovered, hanging underneath a large banana leaf, a whole family of tiny fruit bats suspended upside down neatly in a line! When bananas were ready to pick they came in a bunch of up to eighty at a time - so we would gladly share them round; but before our oranges were properly ripe children would be picking them! The concept of a private garden seemed totally foreign to the majority of Bhutanese! Dot tried for a time to cultivate a small vegetable garden at the back of the bungalow. Not once, but several times in the middle of the night, I had to chase out a huge bull (from who knows where) clad only in my pyjamas (me, not the bull) who was making a midnight feast of our vegetables! Eventually Dot conceded defeat and gave up on the idea.

Jock had grown into a well-fed and handsome animal and was kept busy maintaining his position as top dog among the other dogs around - embarking on a series of serious fights until each vanquished opponent ran off with tail between the legs. There was no special dog food in Bhutan and Jock thrived on a daily diet of rice with a raw egg mixed in - which gave a fine gloss to his coat. Once in a while when we enjoyed either pork or chicken (which were the only meats sometimes available in Bhutan) Jock would get a special treat. We didn't have to worry about bones getting stuck in his throat as he seemed able to wolf down everything with impunity.

Soon Jock was as well known as I was, both around the hospital and on the building site. He established a special relationship with Mandal and if Jock was not at our home he could usually be found lying in the shade near to where Mandal was working; or lying outside Mandal's living quarters. Apart from seeing the occasional *Apso*, domesticated dogs were unusual in Bhutan as most simply run wild and fend for themselves. We had bought for Jock a substantial leather collar which he wore when we took him for a walk on a lead. One day on my way over to the building site I passed some small children playing and was amused to see one child on hands and knees with a piece of string tied round the neck being led by another, saying 'Come on Jock'!

Our domestic life was simple but tough and again made extra demands on Dorothy. For example, though we enjoyed the luxury of water from a tap in the kitchen, it came direct from a jungle stream and every drop had to be boiled to render it fit for human consumption. It was then poured into a two tank filtering system in which it slowly seeped from the top tank into the lower one through stone filter candles. This removed the dirt and sediment so that clear pure drinking water resulted and was then stored in bottles ready to drink. As it was hot at Yebi for much of the year we drank a lot of water; so this purification process had to be maintained constantly to ensure we didn't run out. At certain times of year, the pipes became blocked by berries and other debris coming downstream and then the tap might deliver liquid mud rather than water and the candle filters would require scrubbing every day to keep them from clogging up.

Interruption to the hospital water supply had always been a problem and the hospital cook was frequently seen with spanner in hand or dismantling a section of pipe, doing his best to locate and clear blockages. Preventing any 'Tshering, Dorji or Harry' from taking unilateral action in dealing with interruptions to the water supply, was to prove something of a problem for me. Once the new hospital water distribution system was brought into operation; unqualified interference with the new system had to be discouraged, otherwise all the planning to provide a fair and equitable supply for everyone, could so easily be 'undone' by an unauthorised 'spanner in the works'.

As well as coping with the primitive water supply; once again Dot had to change her whole way of thinking to ensure we had a meal on the table each day. The food situation at Yebi was even more difficult than at Gidakom; as the only supplies normally available here were rice and eggs. For a short time of the year villagers would appear selling bunches of 'fern cross', which was delicious and tasted like asparagus when cooked in oil or butter. Any other food we needed had to be purchased from either the border town of Gelegphu three hours drive south; or from Thimphu when I was making my monthly Project visit there. In the markets at both Gelegphu and Thimphu there was usually a fair selection of fruit and vegetable and in Gelegphu we found out after a while that we could buy chickens. Whenever I visited Thimphu on Project business I would be given a shopping list as long as your arm to buy before I returned.

I had to travel to Thimphu to deliver concrete samples for testing once the concrete work on site was under way; as well as visit various offices to sort out various problems. Travelling as fast as I could on Bhutan's roads the journey took two days driving in each direction; so the return trip took up to a week of my time each month. The last task before returning to Yebi would be to do the shopping. At shop 'No. 7'in Thimphu's main street, imported foodstuff could sometimes be purchased from its enterprising shopkeeper. She'd discovered a niche market among the expatriate community and it was possible to buy various tinned foods there from tuna fish to porridge oats, as well as tea and coffee, and good quality cheese made in Bumthang by the Swiss - if any was still in stock. After a final visit to the open air vegetable market I would return to Yebi with a vehicle laden with food to keep us going - until the next trip.

One thing you dream about working in a place like Bhutan is bacon! The very thought of a few rashers of good Ayrshire bacon sizzling in the frying pan was guaranteed to get the mouth watering. I got very excited on one trip to find tinned bacon from India for sale in shop No 7. I returned to Yebi in triumph bearing several tins. When we emptied the contents of the first into the pan my euphoria dissolved, as it was one solid lump of congealed pork fat and rind! What to do? Dot rendered down the contents anyway, poured off the fat and crisped up the rind to make an edible tasty bite! India also exported tinned oats with which you could make porridge. I opened a new can one morning and a moth flew out! Inside on the top of the oats were the silken threads of the cocoon from which the moth had just hatched - which of course we removed before using the rest! Dot also baked all our bread, apart from the occasional loaf from The Swiss bakery which I might take back as a treat; so on every visit to Thimphu I would fill several buckets with flour to keep us in bread for the next month. The flour required thorough sifting before use to remove the many weevils.

Our friends in Tonbridge were magnificent in their practical and loving support - sending a food parcel *every month* for the three years we were in Bhutan. Receiving these parcels was a great boost to morale as well as our diet. They contained all kinds of tasty treats; from large catering sized jars of Marmite and packets of dehydrated chicken, which Dot used in many ingenious ways; yeast for her bread making; to complete vacuum packed meals from M & S that miraculously survived the long journey from Britain via India, intact. They also sent goodies such as, sweets and 'Angel Delight' - things that man in Bhutan had never yet dreamt of! Most parcels arrived intact and we would open them with the eager anticipation of children unwrapping their Christmas presents.

Sometimes Dot would choose to come with me on a trip to Thimphu as it was especially important for her to keep in touch with her boys in Tonbridge and her daughter in Canada. When we first moved to Yebilaptsa, Thimphu was our nearest place for making phone calls! A young couple Doug and Gliniss from Australia based in Thimphu had a phone in their house and were very kind in letting us use it any time we wanted. When Dot felt she couldn't face the rather daunting journey, she would remain behind at Yebi with Jock as company. I also made quite regular visits to the border town of Gelegphu only three hours drive away, as it had the nearest garage for topping up with diesel; the nearest source of Calor gas; the nearest branch of the Royal Bank of Bhutan which handled the Project account; and the nearest hardware store. Whenever we needed nails, screws, bolts, glass, paint, etc., etc. in fact any hardware for the Project, our nearest supplier was in Gelegphu.

Though the hours of driving on the tortuous roads was demanding it did have its compensations as most of my encounters with wildlife occurred during journeys. Often these were tantalisingly brief and I would just glimpse an animal before it disappeared into the jungle but it was a great thrill to see some of the rarest creatures on earth in their natural habitat. Especially when travelling to Gelegphu through miles of jungle I saw many wild mammals. The black and white Giant Himalayan Squirrel several feet long was fairly common; as were both the Pine Martin and the Rock Martin. On one journey a solitary, rather aggressive looking ape - genre unknown - stood upright on a rock above the road and showed me a fine set of teeth in a rather threatening way as I drove by. On another occasion a whole family of porcupines crossed in front of me - two adults with several young scurrying along behind - all covered in their long wicked looking quills. The endangered Golden Languor monkey was fairly common in this region and I would see troupes quite often on my travels, as well as other primates.

During one winter drive to Thimphu we stopped for a brief rest on reaching the top of the Pele La pass at 3400m to gaze at the Himalaya stretched before us. As I lifted my camera to photograph the magnificent view, a Himalayan Griffon soared up from the valley - the largest bird in the region having an eight-and-a-half foot wingspan - right on cue to complete the picture! Unfortunately, it happened to be the last frame on the film - but what a frame! A little further on the same journey, Dot and I found ourselves looking down on a large airborne flock of Tibetan 'Grandala'. This flock of several hundred birds was made up almost exclusively of males and they have wonderful electric-blue plumage that shimmers as they fly - another memorable sight. On two occasions I saw a Himalayan Red Panda crossing the road, not many miles from Thimphu where the road crosses the Docha la pass. Whilst not nearly as big or spectacular as its cousin the Giant Panda, it was a thrill to see this rather rare animal in its natural habitat.

A Himalayan Griffon seen from the road at Pela la pass

Living in the jungle surrounded by wildlife was not always such pleasure. The whole time we lived at Yebi Dot tolerated a stream of ants marching through her kitchen; they emerged from a small hole in the bamboo wall, walked along a ledge of the wooden framework and then disappeared again through another crack. Provided nothing containing sugar was accessible the ants were no trouble but the smallest trace of sweetness could cause an ant stampede and bring disruption to the kitchen. One evening our living room was invaded by a swarm of countless thousands of flying ants. We were so overwhelmed that we were forced to retire to the bedroom and block the gap at the bottom of the door with a wet towel to prevent them encroaching further. Come the morning when we gingerly opened the bedroom door, all that was left from the nuptial swarm of males and queens the previous night was myriads of discarded tiny wings covering the floor. Our walk in cupboard was used to store the contents of our food parcels and any other food items such as flour, cheese etc. It proved impossible to keep the cupboard free of

179

cockroaches! Just as fast as you dealt with one lot, yet more would appear to take their place! Cockroaches are common throughout Asia and my students at Kharbandi believed that they kept bed bugs under control – at least we never experienced any of those!

Dot loves cooking and even though ingredients were not easily come by we were aware that our diet was much more varied and luxurious compared to that of the construction workers. This was brought home to us when we invited some of the building site staff and Mandal, to a simple buffet meal. Beside piles of rice and vegetables, Dot had managed to concoct a few other simple dishes such as lentil rissoles, scotch pancakes, tuna fish cakes and potato chips – mainly made out of items from our food parcels. She arranged the dishes on the table buffet style so that our guests could help themselves to whatever they fancied. Dear Mandal my carpenter looked at this table of simple food and said to me quietly and in a voice that conveyed a genuine sense of wonder, *'My! Seven items'!* It was quite evident that never before had he seen such a spread. It brought home to me the enormous gulf between 'the haves' like ourselves, and 'the have not's' of this world. Now, whenever I see a buffet table laden with food I invariably think of dear Mandal and his reaction - *'My! Seven items'.* To this day I choke up at the memory and probably from an underlying guilt at just how much we take the good life for granted.

Being a strictly Buddhist country, the killing of animals for food is generally forbidden so fresh meat was only an occasional luxury. For some peculiar religious reason, in Bhutan pigs and chicken are excluded from this prohibition! On special occasions one of the hospital staff would kill a domestic pig and then we might enjoy fresh pork - provided that is we learned in time that it was being sold and was able to buy a piece before it was all snapped up. The usual alert that told you pork might be available that day was very loud squealing that could be heard clearly from every corner of the hospital compound as the pig was slaughtered. Only if you were quick enough in finding out whose pig it was and you got there soon enough, might you get a piece.

Another occasional variation to our diet was when Mandal brought us fish. He was a keen fisherman and might spend his Saturday afternoon off work, down in the Mangde Chhu river fishing. I say 'in' the river because when he fished he would be stood up to the waist in water holding a long bamboo cane, from the top end of which would be tied a length of fishing line. At the lower end of the line was a noose, fashioned in such a way as to hold a piece of breadfruit at its centre. It was dangled in the fast flowing river and fish were literally lassoed when they swam into the noose to take the bait and were then jerked out of the water. We thoroughly enjoyed the large river trout which Mandal brought to us from time to time. You needed a permit to fish in Bhutan and no fishing at all was permitted on certain days of the month, or at any time within sight of a monastery - as fishing is offensive to a monk.

Before we'd discovered the chicken farm in Gelegphu; for our first Christmas dinner at Yebi I managed to purchase two chickens via Thinley, the Bhutanese 'fix it' specialist who worked for the contractor. He obtained (at a price!) two cockerels from a villager, and the rather lean birds were delivered still alive and crowing in time for Christmas dinner. Fortunately, in my youth we had kept chicken, so I knew how to kill, pluck, draw and clean one. The cockerels were duly 'dispatched' and prepared for the pot and though they proved to be a bit on the tough side, we appreciated that special Christmas treat as much if not more than any Christmas turkey we have had since.

Most people in Bhutan cook with the aid of a simple wood fired clay oven, actually built on the floor of a house. Dot cooked on a brand new Calor gas stove, with three top burners, a grill and an oven; which I purchased in Thimphu. This was the height of domestic sophistication in Bhutan, but the down side was that the Calor gas cylinders required were imported from India and always in short supply. Spare cylinders were strictly rationed to just one per household and could only be obtained from a single source in either Gelegphu or Thimphu. This restriction was fine if you were living in one of those places, but here in the back of beyond it was certainly not adequate to ensure you didn't run out of gas; especially when you were baking your bread as well as cooking meals by gas! After some time and by pleading our cause, we eventually managed to obtain a spare from *both* supply centres, which gave us the reserve needed.

Dot was encouraged by TLM to employ a Bhutanese to help in the home so that indirectly the local economy would be boosted – not that Dot was exactly run off her feet in keeping our bungalow clean! She employed the wife of one of the hospital cleaners who proved to be extremely reliable and diligent. Though she'd not had the benefit of formal education beyond primary level, she was an intelligent and able young woman. Promptly at eight each morning she appeared ready for work with her baby daughter tied to her back. Though her English was very limited and Dot's

Kengkha' (the local language in the Yebi area) non-existent, they got along just fine and soon developed a great fondness for one another. She was keen to learn any new skill that Dot could teach her, such as baking bread and making scotch pancakes - one of Dot's specialities. Like most women in Bhutan she was a capable weaver, whereas Dot had always been an enthusiastic knitter. She was keen to learn how to knit and amazed us at how easily she was able to produce quite involved knitted garments without the aid of a printed pattern. One day Dot showed her a picture of an Aran sweater and demonstrated how to knit the cable down the front. She went away with wool and needles and not many days later came back with a complete sweater front.

Bhutanese women produce the most beautiful intricately woven and quality cloth on basic hand looms; usually a simple affair requiring the weaver to sit on the floor facing the wall on which the loom is fastened; the cloth being tensioned by a rope from a wooden bar going round the weavers' lower back. To weave sufficient cloth for a traditional 'kho' for a man or a 'kira' for a woman is many weeks of work. Different patterns are produced in the various regions of Bhutan and their intricate designs are woven without anything written down. The skill of weaving and the different designs are passed down from mother to daughter through successive generations purely by example. This natural ability in weaving may explain how Dot's helper mastered the new skill of knitting so readily – without any pattern.

Dot had plenty of time to knit as she had few official duties other than to keep me 'firing on all cylinders' which she did very well. When given the opportunity she made herself useful in other ways. Children's clothes were sent by supporters of the Leprosy Mission especially for new born babies and Dot helped to keep the children's clothing store in order. Also, when lessons at the local school were over for the day, the daughter of one hospital staff member came to Dot for help with her English. By the time we left Yebi her English was much improved but spoken with a distinctly Scottish accent!

When there was time to relax we listened to the BBC World Service on the short wave radio and this was a valued link with home; keeping us in touch with the national and international news. Dot also enjoyed listening to music and the afternoon plays. Like many ex-pats I also kept up to date on current affairs by receiving the special airmail edition of the 'Manchester Guardian' each week - though most times it was old news by the time it reached us at Yebi! A small selection of good books had been left behind by the English nursing staff who had worked there and these were appreciated by us both.

Any ex-patriot working in Bhutan had a visitor quota of two people per year; as the Royal Government was concerned about limiting the influence of the outside world on Bhutan's culture, which had remained unchanged for centuries. We had just four guests during our three years in Bhutan! Any visitor we invited was not expected to pay the tourist rate when they got there but it was still expensive to come to Bhutan from Britain. Just in driving from the airport over to Yebi and back again took four precious days of any visit, but at Christmas 1992 my son and his wife came to stay first with Alison at Gidakom and then with us at Yebi. They were newly married and it was good for them to be able to experience Bhutan and it gave them a better appreciation of Alison's nursing work and situation at Gidakom and our very different situation at Yebilaptsa.

The only down side to the visit, was when we received a radio message to say their London flat had been burgled! It was vital that they put an immediate block on the further use of any credit and debit cards, etc. that may have been stolen; so we had to get to the nearest telephone immediately. My son and I set off in the middle of the afternoon to drive four hours north to Trongsa where a telephone had recently been installed. This is a narrow and little used road and for many miles passes through forest-covered mountainside. Being December the days were short and we were still an hour's drive from Trongsa as the light began to fail. As we rounded a bend, just twenty yards ahead two huge saucer-like eyes reflected the light from our headlights back at us, out of the gloom. A very large big-cat – possibly a mountain puma, stood directly in our path and its body plus tail stretched across the road. It barely paused to look at our approaching vehicle before walking over the outer edge of the road and disappearing immediately into the forest below. When we reached our Tibetan guest house and reported what we'd seen, Ama said, 'Oh yes, just a few weeks ago one jumped on to the cab of a lorry and almost frightened its driver to death!' I had never seen such a huge, truly wild big-cat before, and was thankful it had been safely from the inside of a vehicle!

Before they returned to Britain we took a weekend break and all stayed together for a couple of nights in the comparative luxury of the Swiss Guest house in Bumthang. Even at the Guest House you had to be aware of the possible danger from wildlife. Black bears are common in this region and every year one or two attacks on humans take place in Bhutan -

some resulting in horrific injuries; but during all my time in Bhutan I never saw a Black Bear even at a distance. On one occasion Dot and I were staying at the Swiss Guest House and she needed to use the toilet which was outside, in the middle of the night. To ensure her safety I had to accompany her, and as I stood guard keeping an eye open for bears a large wild cat walked by the door of the latrine! From the inside Dot only saw a shadow pass across the gap at the bottom of the door but fortunately was unaware that a potentially dangerous wild animal was passing within a few feet of her!

Because Bhutan is such a devoutly Buddhist country where killing anything is regarded as a great sin, there is still an abundance of wildlife; and no doubt many wild animals live side by side with human neighbours largely unobserved and untroubled. When during one of my many visits to her guesthouse in Trongsa, I suggested that they used a fly killer in the kitchen to keep down the abundant fly population that always seemed to be around where the guests ate: Ama the Tibetan hotel keeper was absolutely horrified!

Our next guest was a friend from home who in the course of his high profile position in the City of London travelled to places all over the developed world. He stood up to the tortuous travelling very well but it concerned us that he was unusually quiet. As this was somewhat out of character we wondered if anything was wrong. It was only after our return to Britain that he confided he was 'bowled over' by the whole experience! Bhutan was so different to the many other countries he'd visited. During his stay he and I trekked for a day to a village high on the mountain opposite Yebi - which I had only seen in the distance from the back of our bungalow but had never visited. It was a good day's strenuous walking which we thoroughly enjoyed. As Project Manager I had little time off to get away to walk but this day brought home to me the enormous effort that must be involved in conducting the leprosy survey programme in Bhutan; when every village however remote is visited, to examine every person in the population for any early signs of leprosy – every year!

During my absence an unfortunate accident took place. Mandal slipped and fell from the roof where he was working and was admitted to the hospital. There was no easy way of contacting us but Dot tried by hanging out an improvised banner that read '**HELP, PLEASE RETURN HOME**' hoping we would see this **SOS** from the mountainside opposite. We didn't; but thankfully Mandal though concussed, bruised and shaken up, didn't suffer any broken bones and quickly made a full recovery.

We would have loved more family and friends to have come; but the cost, the time and the difficult journey involved in getting to Yebi put most people off from seriously considering it. We especially regret that Dot's children didn't come to Bhutan and they regret missing out on what would have been the experience of a lifetime.

Our last guest was Gottfried Riedel who came toward the end of the Project on a semi - official trip on behalf of The Leprosy Mission International and the German wing of the Mission responsible for the Project funding. It was good to see him again and Gottfried was thrilled with the new and vastly improved facilities already completed at Yebi.

Dot and I made two short visits back to Britain for the marriage of two of our children. During summer 1992 my son was married; then the following summer Dot's daughter was also married. These home visits made welcome breaks when we were able to spend time with our children and generally catch up with wider family and friends; as well as enjoy a welcome break from the pressure of the Project work and the isolation at Yebilaptsa.

Going home during the British summer meant we escaped some of the worst weather at Yebi, because it was the time of monsoon. Any building work was practically halted anyway, as the rainfall is so intense the ground on site is waterlogged; and the roads might well be blocked by landslides preventing delivery of materials. While we were in Britain and the Project almost at a standstill, I left my counterpart Deepak in charge; and by arrangement many of the Project workers also went home to visit family in Assam and West Bengal. At the end of our home visits Dot stayed on in Britain for a few weeks longer; while I returned to Bhutan alone to ensure that construction work got under way again as soon as conditions allowed. It was when I was at Yebi without Dot that the M & S vacuum packed meals from our food parcels came into their own! During those weeks I was largely fending for myself and survived quite well on a vacuum packed meal per day - until Dot's very welcome return!

The drive from Paro to Yebilaptsa at this time of year was extremely difficult. There were long stretches of road still to be surfaced and the sea of mud caused even a 4 X 4 to slew all over the place. You never knew when or where the road might be blocked by landslips and in the absence of any telephone service you seldom learnt about a landslide until you actually reached it. Looking back, I wonder just how I managed the return journey on my Bajaj scooter at the start of monsoon without any serious mishap!

Returning on my own to Yebi after our first trip home, I made good progress until on the road south about 30 kilometres beyond Trongsa I was brought to an unexpected halt at a large concrete bridge some thirty metres long (built by the Indian Army) and spanning a very steeply inclined mountain stream. The road was closed off and a group of men hovered nearby – seemingly doing very little. When I went over to investigate I was amazed to see that this huge reinforced concrete bridge weighing hundreds of tons, had somehow been pushed sideways by more than a metre and no longer lined up with the road at each end! Seemingly, the stream running under the bridge is fed from a high altitude lake far above. Following a particularly heavy cloudburst the lower end of the lake had burst; sending a huge torrent of water and debris careering down the mountainside. A rock the size of a house had bounced off the bed of the stream and struck the underside of the bridge with such momentum and force it had literally punched the whole bridge out of alignment! The under side in the middle bore testament to this, as it was a tangled mess of exposed steel reinforcing rods with odd lumps of concrete attached – dangling in midair above the river bed!

There was no other way I knew that I could get to Yebi without obtaining a visa to travel through Assam; as the only alternative route to Yebi at that time was from Phunsholing, through Assam to Gelegphu; and so approaching Yebi from the south. This would involve a two-day drive back to Phuentsholing; plus, a further day or two driving from Phuentsholing to Yebi – and who knows how long in between, obtaining a permit to travel through this sensitive

189

military area of India – if I could obtain one! I explained my predicament to the man in charge and asked permission to drive across the damaged bridge but he was adamant that I could not - it was a real impasse. After a long discussion I was told to speak to the Chief Roads Engineer who was now in Trongsa! I returned to Trongsa only to find that the Chief Engineer had returned to the bridge and must have passed me on route! Back I travelled and caught up with him at last and once more engaged in a protracted discussion. Finally, he gave me permission to cross - at my own risk. We built a ramp of soil and planks so that I could drive up onto the damaged and now elevated bridge - as it had also been lifted by the force of the impact about a foot above road level. Gingerly I drove up the makeshift ramp and across the damaged bridge and to safety onto the road once more on the other side, via a similar ramp.

A few weeks later I had the problem of reaching Paro to meet Dot when her flight arrived - as the road via Trongsa was still closed to traffic. My only option was to attempt to travel via an unmade road which the hospital staff told me was under construction just inside the southern border with India but which was far from complete. This route meant travelling through the area of conflict between the Nepali Bhutanese and Bhutan's army and was closed to foreigners. Fortunately, I had a special permit to travel through this region because I needed to make business trips to Gelegphu.

After passing through Gelegphu I discovered the new route crossed a wide and normally shallow river at a fording place and no bridge had been built yet. Though the monsoon was over the river still flowed fairly full and again the driving conditions demonstrated the absolute necessity of having a diesel powered 4 x 4. All went well until I was in the very middle of the river where the water was at its deepest and I felt the vehicle begin to lift! Water was over the top of the door cill and I had visions of floating helplessly down river into India - but there was no turning back. For what seemed to be for ever, but was probably only a minute or two, I fought to keep the vehicle facing forward as it was being pushed sideways by the current; hoping against hope that the tyres would somehow grip on the river bed. Suddenly they took hold and the vehicle moved toward the far bank and into shallower water. I heaved a sigh of relief at deliverance from yet another potentially nasty situation.

The rest of my journey passed without incident and I regained my usual route at the Bailey bridge at Wangdi and so was able to meet Dot on her arrival at Paro as arranged. After completing business in Thimphu and we had shopped for food we were ready to return to Yebi again. News reached us that the damaged bridge near Trongsa had now been declared safe for light vehicles and so we returned on our normal route.

The following summer after our second trip home, I again returned ahead of Dot. Our reunion on this occasion was memorable for a reason neither of us can forget. I drove this time without difficulty to Paro to meet the flight on which Dot was due, flying in from Delhi via Kathmandu. Though visibility was good and there was no obvious reason for delay her plane failed to arrive. After a long time of waiting we were eventually told by airport staff there had been a plane crash in Nepal and no flight would be arriving in Paro that day. They had no further information to give and we were simply asked to come back next morning. In the absence of news, I spent an extremely anxious night in Paro wondering what could have happened. When the airport opened next day I was very relieved to be told that the Druk Air flight had been held overnight in Kathmandu but should be arriving sometime that day, weather permitting. Dot eventually arrived safely and only then I learned that the Pakistan Airlines flight immediately in front of Dots, in making its final approach at Kathmandu had crashed into the side of a mountain. Dot had seen the plume of smoke rising from the crash as her plane followed in to land. We learned later that more than 230 people on board had all perished.

We had to travel so much by air and by road over the duration of the Project and we were truly thankful not to be involved in any kind of accident. Travelling on Bhutan's roads was always potentially dangerous and you had to anticipate danger round every bend. Twice when being driven in other people's vehicles we came very close to going over the edge of the road – and on both occasions found ourselves staring down a near vertical drop to almost certain death. Knowing that during the Project I would be driving thousands of kilometres, I was much more comfortable driving myself than employing a driver - as he might well have never taken a driving test!

I tried to minimise the risk by avoiding night driving as far as possible but there was one journey from Yebi to the border town of Gelegphu that I had no choice but to make in the middle of the night. It was during the conflict in the south between Government troops and the so called guerrilla fighters or 'anti-nationals' as they were termed. I had made this journey often during the day but never at night, and travelling through this area was now particularly risky. The town of Gelegphu itself was under a night time curfew so even legitimate travel came to a complete standstill after dark.

A medical emergency arose at Yebi but the vehicle which would have normally been used for transporting a patient, was already away on a leprosy control survey; so the Project vehicle was the only one available. A pregnant woman due to give birth any time soon was experiencing serious complications. I was told that unless she could be transferred to the larger and better equipped hospital at Gelegphu immediately, she might well die before morning. With a male midwife in the passenger seat beside me; the patient lying across the back seat, and her husband kneeling behind her in the luggage space holding up an intravenous drip; we set out well after ten o'clock on the three-hour drive south on a lovely night with a full moon shining high above the forested hilltops.

The road south from Yebi climbs steadily for several miles until levelling out through a forested pass. It then descends through a particularly tortuous section cut through very difficult terrain with jungle below the road and a rock face on the inside. We were only too aware of the guerrilla fighting that had been taking place in this area for the past few years and the danger of being hijacked. When we came to a barrier of earth and debris blocking the road, we immediately wondered whether it might be an ambush. We had little choice but to get out and clear the road sufficiently and as quickly as we could, to allow the vehicle through.

After an anxious holdup we resumed our journey south, the route then passing through an extensively cultivated area. Sadly, the once fertile fields were now all lying fallow and several villages formerly home to Nepali Bhutanese, were totally deserted as their occupants had been evicted from Bhutan. Once more we entered a wild uncultivated area where the road is hewn from a rock face and there was thick bamboo jungle below us. Again we were forced to a halt, this time by a large tree trunk blocking the full width of the road. We had heard of this tactic being used to stop and ambush vehicles so it was very scary to be stood in the middle of a lonely road in the dark in such a vulnerable location; knowing full well that people were getting high jacked in situations like this. Leaving the husband to care for his sick wife; the male nurse and I heaved and strained to swivel the sizable tree trunk around sufficiently to be able to drive by one end. We did eventually manage to shift it but only with great difficulty and so continued on to deliver our patient – hopefully to hospital and not in the back of the vehicle!

All our excitement was not over! Before reaching the town of Gelegphu the road crosses a major river on a suspension bridge - either side of which was an army check post where vehicles are stopped and passengers scrutinised. When we arrived at the barrier in the dead of night it was alarming to find ourselves looking down the barrel of a machine gun, stuck out from a hole in the side of a heavily sand-bagged army post. The guards were obviously on full alert and feeling just as vulnerable as we were but having the definite advantage of being armed! Calling out at the top of my voice I hastily reassured whoever was inside, that we posed no threat; just in case they had any tendency to be trigger happy. After explaining our reason for being on the road at what was now past midnight, we were cautiously inspected and allowed to proceed.
Once again on the far side of the bridge we were put through

a repeat performance - again at gun point. Having survived so far we reached the town, which being under curfew was deathly quiet and its streets deserted except for stray dogs. We thought our troubles were over and that we had made it safely through - but there was one obstacle remaining that we'd not thought of. The main army barracks was next door to the hospital and of course - it was also on full alert! For the third time that night we found ourselves looking down the business end of a machine gun and had to explain ourselves, before at last being allowed into the hospital compound to hand over our patient.

The patient's husband and the male nurse were to remain at the hospital with the patient, so having fulfilled my duty as driver I left them to look for somewhere I could spend the rest of the night. All the places for 'fooding and lodging' were of course locked and shuttered and no-one would open a door this time of night. I had no desire to hang about in Gelegphu until dawn so I decided I might as well begin my drive back to Yebi as spend what was left of the night trying to sleep in the vehicle. Thankfully the return journey went without incident - apart that is from an encounter with a rather special nocturnal animal the like of which I had never seen before!

It was still completely dark when I reached a point on the route where the road is cut from an overhanging rock face and high overhead a number of large wild bee nests hung suspended - a common enough sight in southern Bhutan. On previous daytime trips I had seen Rock Martins at this location coming down from above, obviously having raided the nests for honey. As I now approached, a large squirrel-like mammal dropped just in front of the vehicle. It paused on a rock at the side of the road in the full beam of my headlights for what seemed like several minutes, before launching itself into the jungle below. As it sat in the headlight for quite a time I had a very good look at it. It was an intriguing animal considerably larger than a squirrel and its fur looked black - apart from two large and very distinct perfect circles of white - one on its back and the other on the visible underside of the tail; which it held upright behind its body in a typically squirrel-like posture. Only many years later did someone identify it for me as most probably a rare Red and White Giant Flying Squirrel - an animal now restricted to a small area of Assam and this part of southern Bhutan. Having a glimpse of this rare nocturnal animal which I had never seen before made the whole scary adventure for me doubly worthwhile.

During one of my daytime business trips to Gelegphu, the considerable impact of the ethnic strife in the south on the lives of many ordinary Bhutanese was brought home to me by a chance meeting. My last stop before starting out on the return journey to Yebi was the fuel station on the outskirts of town. As I was topping up my tank with diesel I was approached by an ex-student from Kharbandi who I had not seen for at least five years. I was delighted to meet him and I was all set for a long chat; but he cut me short, saying: "I just wanted to say hello but I mustn't stay to talk with you as I might be being watched and could get into trouble for speaking with a foreigner!" This ex-student was a southern Bhutanese of Nepali descent! Though he'd said so little, his nervous demeanour left me in no doubt that he was genuinely scared of possible repercussions should he be seen and reported for speaking with me. Later on I was to discover more of what was going on behind the scenes.

Chapter 14
Building Yebilaptsa Hospital

The new hospital at Yebilaptsa was an example of good international cooperation. The Project was initiated by The Leprosy Mission which is itself multinational. Most of the funding came from Germany but with an additional top-up from the people of the Channel Islands. Its architect Rob Fielding and myself the Project Manager, are both British; the site manager Nema was Nepalese; the site engineer Mandal came from India; and Thinley the 'quartermaster' responsible for obtaining everything from rice and eggs to stone and sand, was Bhutanese. The main labour force including my carpenter Mandal came from West Bengal and Assam in India. The electricity supply was courtesy of the Japanese using Filipino labour; the hospital electrification was overseen by Pema Gyeltshen a Bhutanese; and the approach road was built by the Indian army using Nepali labour. All the contracting companies involved were owned and managed by Bhutanese. I also received useful help and advice along the way from an Australian, a New Zealander, a Swiss, and a Dutchman!

The **'Yebilaptsa Hospital Expansion'** would comprise ....

An **Operating Theatre and Delivery Suite** with changing and linen rooms, sluices and a **Recovery Room**.
Four General Wards each with toilets and showers (accessible to wheel chair users).
Four two-bed **Intensive Nursing Units** each with en-suite shower and toilet facilities.
A Nursing Station including **Matrons Office**; drug

preparation area; and a **Linen Store**.

A '**Dirty Surgery' Room** for minor medical procedures.

A **Physiotherapy Room and Office**

In addition:-

Six further **Staff Living Quarters** were to be built.

A **Garage** for three 4 x 4 hospital vehicles, complete with inspection pit.

A new **Hospital Kitchen** with food preparation area, wood store, food store and servery.

The original hospital buildings were to be renovated and modified to provide upgraded facilities for: a **Dentistry; Out Patients Clinic; Health Education Classroom; improved X-ray facility; Pharmacy; Superintendents Office** and **Leprosy Control Room**.

The old kitchen was to be converted into a **Laundry** with a secure covered drying area.

A new **water supply system** for both the hospital and its staff quarters was required.

Proper **drainage and sewage systems** were to be installed.

Septic tanks and soak-away chambers were to be provided.

On completion of a nearby hydro-electric power project carried out by the Japanese, **Electrification** of both the hospital and staff quarters would also be carried out.

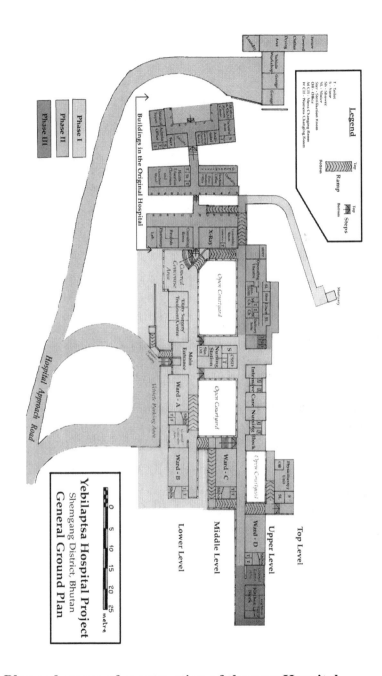

Planned stages of construction of the new Hospital

199

The hillside on which the hospital was built sloped and was thickly wooded. Our first task was to clear the new hospital site but the trees immediately above this area were to be left in situ as these were vitally important in holding the top soil in place, which might otherwise silt up the drainage and sewage systems of the new hospital. I awoke one Sunday morning to the sound of a chain saw when no work should have been happening on site: to discover to my horror that the Forestry Department had ordered the felling of these trees also. It was with some difficulty that I persuaded the forestry men who spoke no English that unless they stopped work it would have disastrous consequences for the new hospital. In the absence of a telephone, the next day I drove 30 kilometres to Zhemgang and consulted the local Dzongda who did understand my concern and issued an order that the felling be cancelled.

Before the foundations could be dug it was necessary to chemically treat the whole site to deter termites. Termites abound in the jungle area of southern Bhutan and without protective chemical treatment they would given time eat their way through the woodwork of the new hospital, just as they had done through the window frames at Kharbandi College! A specialist for this work was brought up from India - a man with a large military moustache and a big personality to match! He was very good at giving orders to those detailed to actually carry out the treatment, and whilst the whole site was sprayed with a very pungent smelling chemical, I noticed he stood well clear. After this, the first foundation trenches were dug - by hand of course. Steel reinforcing rods were prepared and placed in position that would give the strength needed for the framework to withstand earth tremors; as Bhutan being in the Himalayas, the earth's youngest mountain chain, is in an active earthquake zone.

I was impressed at how carefully every building was exactly marked out by the Indian civil engineer Sadasib Mandal employed by the contractor, using theodolite and level. He always asked me to double check his work but there was never an occasion when his measurements were not absolutely correct. He didn't know that my background training was in shipbuilding and naval architecture and not in civil engineering! Working with a theodolite would certainly have been outside my comfort zone but after returning home from Bhutan in 1987 I had taught Mathematics to student surveyors, and this had required me to take a crash course in the use of a theodolite and level – an experience which now proved to be invaluable!

We soon discovered that very deep top soil had accumulated at this site over decades and necessitated excavating exceptionally deep foundation trenches etc. When later on a hole was dug to house the Operating Theatre septic tank, it was five metres deep and we were still in top soil! All of the excavation was carried out by hand! The only mechanical aids were a small and well used diesel driven cement mixer; a diesel driven vibrator for compacting concrete; and later after an electricity supply was provided, an electric floor grinder and polisher was employed in finishing the surface of the marble chip concrete floors.

The foundations, main pillars and lintel band round the top of the walls of every building was of reinforced concrete, to provide a flexible framework that would give resistance to total collapse in the event of an earthquake; so a lot of concrete was mixed and poured. Wheel barrows were unknown in

Bhutan so this considerable volume of concrete was transferred from the mixer to where it was needed in shallow circular metal pans carried on the heads of the labourers, working in a continuous human chain. The cement mixer was made in India and was powered by a diesel engine; the mixing drum being rotated via rather vulnerable unguarded cast iron gearing. Disaster struck one day, when a stone got caught in the gears and one of the cast iron wheels fractured into three pieces. The site foreman informed me that a replacement would have to be obtained from India and would take at least a month! I knew that a month might mean anything up to three months! What to do? It's the kind of dilemma you face working in the back of beyond.

Desperate situations call for unusual solutions! Having worked in shipbuilding I knew how durable and strong good plywood can be. One of Bhutan's first factories was for the manufacture of quality plywood and we had some 12mm ply on site. Much to the surprise of the work force who were not used to seeing a boss actually working with his hands, I cut out a sandwich of plywood to hold the broken pieces of gearwheel together - the layers all firmly glued and screwed to one another. We then reassembled the mixer and the 'gearwheel sandwich' kept it working for two more weeks until the constant vibration loosened the screws and caused the broken gear to fail to mesh properly. It then had to be removed; the ply re-glued and re-screwed before serving us for a further two weeks. In this way we maintained the building schedule and continued mixing concrete until eventually the replacement gear arrived.

Our bungalow (and my office) was only about a hundred yards from the building site so I didn't have far to travel to work each day! Typically, on a weekday, I would start from early morning working on layout drawings; then following breakfast at eight, would make my first site visit to discuss with the foreman the work planned for that day. Another spell of office work followed, dealing with correspondence and accounts, etc. as well as more drawing work. Toward the end of the morning I might make a site visit to check on progress, before Dot and I enjoyed lunch together. Afternoons followed a similar pattern and before work finished on site at five, the foreman and I would inspect whatever work had been accomplished that day. This routine meant that about half my time was spent in the office and half reviewing and resolving practical problems and monitoring progress on site. There was never any conflict in having my office within our living quarters and it was very convenient if I was needed to look at something urgently. The senior Asian staff always respected our privacy and there was never any problem living this close to the site.

Whenever concrete was being mixed and poured I would make an unannounced visit to the site, confiscate one of the metal dishes of concrete at random from a labourer, and pour its contents into a standard concrete sampling mould. It was carefully recorded and numbered so that I could identify exactly what section of concrete it came from. Samples were locked away for a month to cure - to reach their full strength. Then once a month I would drive to Thimphu, the vehicle loaded down with dozens of concrete cubes to be tested in the Roads Laboratory; the only lab in Bhutan equipped for carrying out the test. Unavoidably, more than six weeks might elapse between the concrete sample being collected on site and getting the test result from the lab; by which time the building work would have advanced somewhat. It was my hope that no sample would ever fail!

The time and trouble taken carrying out these checks was very necessary. On a project elsewhere in Bhutan it had been discovered that their cement had been mixed with some worthless white powder and the resulting concrete considerably weakened as a consequence. The fact that I took concrete samples and had them tested, served to warn the contractor that any deficiency in strength was likely to be discovered. The mica content of the sand used and the speed with which newly poured concrete dries out, can also affect the strength of the concrete. Prior to the monsoon it got progressively hotter and this meant that special measures had to be taken to prevent newly cast concrete from drying out too quickly. When the vertical wooden shuttering was removed exposing the new concrete, each pillar would be wrapped with sacking, and a 'pani walla' (water carrier) equipped with a bucket of water and a tin can, spent all day going round the site keeping the sacking wet. Naturally he was nick-named Gunga Din!

Between the concrete columns the walls were built of brick - rather poor looking bricks imported from India that looked as if they were individually hand made rather than cast in a mould - but I was assured they were the best available. 'Butterfly Irons' fixed at intervals into the reinforcing steelwork and protruding from the concrete vertical columns; provided a proper structural tie between the brick wall and the adjoining pillars. The window and door units were similarly tied in to the main structure by galvanised iron linkages. The window frames rested on reinforced concrete window cills cast on site.

The intricate detail of the Bhutanese style wood frames around door and window openings was displayed to best advantage by setting them against a plain cement plaster finish. On the other hand, plain walls without any door or windows openings, together with the steps connecting different levels and the low retaining walls; were all finished with a facing of dressed natural stone which provided a pleasant contrast.

Disruptions on the road such as landslips could interrupt the work, as apart from timber all other raw materials came from a distance. The cement came from Bhutan's only cement factory in western Bhutan two days' drive away; sand was dug from a river bed near Gelegphu three hours away; stone was quarried direct from a road side rock face between Trongsa and Zhemgang just two hours away; plywood for the ceilings came from Bhutan's plywood factory at Gedu in western Bhutan three days' drive away; bricks and steel were imported from India; as was galvanised corrugated iron sheeting. All the fixtures and fittings, including glass for the windows, paint, screws, etc. etc., for completing the buildings, were all obtained from India through a merchant in Gelegphu.

Timber was the one material we did not have to transport from a distance, as a saw mill was situated in the nearby village of Tintinbi. The Bhutanese manager at the mill was a likable and cooperative man and did his best to keep up with our demands. The mill was equipped with a diesel powered band saw which cut timber down to the size we required from well seasoned logs. The mill supplied almost all the timber we required - which was considerable, especially for the roof trusses and purlins. During the whole construction period we experienced very little delay in the delivery of timber.

In spite of my limited experience of civil building work, much to my surprise I still found on occasions I knew more than the contractor - when for example we reached DPC (damp proof course) level on the first buildings. They had never seen, let alone installed a damp course before - such a refinement was unknown in Bhutan at that time. After explaining what a DPC was for, the materials were purchased from India and I demonstrated how to incorporate it into the building. They only had to be shown once and then followed the instructions meticulously. Confirmation of the effectiveness of the DPC came unexpectedly when much later on in the Project a labourer was admitted as a patient to one of the new wards during the monsoon. He was quite amazed to see for himself that even though it was very wet outside there was not a trace of water seeping up through the floor from below - which he had always been accustomed to in the past!

The Garage was the first building on site to be ready for roofing and a lorry load of slate (the only lorry load as it turned out) arrived from the quarry near Wangdi together with a trained roofer. The roofer just happened to be there when Dorothy put on the simple buffet supper for some of the construction staff - so we also invited him. We had a number of games and puzzles the like of which none of our guests had seen before; they included several consisting of stiff interlocking pieces of foam rubber that fitted together to form a flat rectangle but which could be reconfigured to form a cube. This could only be done successfully in one way and Deepak my counterpart, Nima the site foreman, and Mandal the site engineer all tried but failed to solve any of the puzzles. The Roofer who had had no formal education took each one and solved it without too much trouble displaying a well developed innate spatial ability. What might he have achieved had he received an education? Building the roof of the hospital posed quite a challenge as the various individual buildings were sited at four different levels up the hillside; yet the roof needed to be continuous throughout the hospital. My carpenter Profulla proved equal to the task and was responsible for the whole roof construction. Once the prototype of any particular roof truss had been made with my guidance, Mandal would then produce whatever number of that pattern was required.

The timber wall plate, to which the roof trusses are fixed, was secured to the lintel by steel bolts set into the concrete. This timber wall plate had to be carefully drilled to align with the bolts and recessed to accommodate the fixing nuts. To help Mandal in this task I took out from Britain a traditional carpenter's brace together with an adjustable drill bit. Though this type of brace is now almost obsolete in Britain the Asian carpenters crowded round to watch with great interest as Mandal effortlessly drilled the required holes. They had never seen one of these before and their usual method for drilling holes was crude and time consuming by comparison using a kind of bow and spindle!

There were no cranes on site - in fact the only crane I ever saw in Bhutan was a Black-Necked one that had flown from Tibet! When the wall plate was finished, the many heavy roof trusses had to be manually lifted into place; a task involving the whole labour force and requiring very careful coordination. Thankfully, due to good control by Nima the foreman at ground level, and by carpenter Mandal at wall top level, this heavy and dangerous job was completed without mishap.

As Yarkey Construction had no one skilled in glass cutting; Mandal who had some previous experience, was given the considerable task of cutting and fitting the dozens of panes of glass into the many windows and skylights. I took a diamond glass cutter out from the UK to help him do the job and the glass was ordered through the ironmonger in Gelegphu. Transporting it back to Yebi involved a long journey driving at a snails pace on the tortuous and less than perfect road from Gelegphu. The glass was stacked edge on from one side to the other across the back of the Project vehicle with its rear seat removed; using hospital blankets as padding on either side. I had not appreciated the considerable weight of glass! It was by far the heaviest load the Suzuki was ever to carry - heavier by far than the concrete test samples! I drove back trying my best to avoid all the potholes, and the normal three-hour journey took more like five.

All sorts of hardware items that we take for granted and are freely available in the UK, were unobtainable in either Bhutan or India. At the end of one home leave I returned with an assortment of things packed in a large fibre suitcase. I was called over the Tannoy at Heathrow to report to Security who asked me to open the suitcase. Inside was a Black & Decker workbench (for Mandal); four hydraulic door closers (for the Operating Theatre); several sets of large castors (for hospital trolleys); plus, a fishing rod and hooks (for one of the hospital staff); as well as the diamond glass cutter and carpenters brace and bit, plus other smaller items. This conglomeration must have had the security staff truly baffled as it passed through the airport security X- ray machine!

Whilst one Phase of the building programme was taking shape, my counterpart Deepak and I were busy preparing the drawings, estimates etc., for the next Phase. Deepak had joined me as soon as construction work began and we worked closely together. He was often left in charge when I was away in Thimphu or Gelegphu and he produced many of the detailed drawings for the plumbing and sanitary installations in showers, toilets, sluice rooms, etc. Deepak was meticulous in his draughtsmanship and the work he did made a valuable contribution to the Project, as well as giving him experience on which he could draw in future. Near the end of the Project, I gave him increased responsibility and made him wholly responsible for specific areas on which he worked largely unaided, not only to give him experience but also for his personal satisfaction.

On every trip to Thimphu with the concrete samples I would also take the latest drawings for photocopying: to provide the contractors with the plans they needed; for the records of the International Leprosy Mission Office in London; and as part of my progress report for the German donor. My quarterly donor reports had to include photographs to show building progress since the previous quarter. There were no digital cameras, so the latest photos had to be developed and printed in the one shop in Thimphu able to offer this service. From the drawings, written reports, photos and accounts, the donor was able to monitor progress and in effect audit the payments made to the Contractor.

The significantly enlarged hospital required a new water distribution system and my experience of the shared water supply at Kharbandi now proved invaluable when designing the new system for Yebi. The original hospital supply came from a mountain stream into a holding tank and was then piped down through the jungle for over half a kilometre. This supply had been adequate for the original hospital and its staff quarters (in quantity if not in quality) but would not be sufficient for the enlarged hospital. Once again I was grateful for good expert advice; this time given by a young Dutch water engineer Tjakko, living nearby in Zhemgang and working for 'Save the Children'.

We struggled up through the jungle to the top of the pipeline and then discovered that another holding tank had been built higher up the stream and a second pipe installed to supply a new school under construction! In the same way as the water supply at Kharbandi had been plagiarised by other users; so now the Yebi hospital supply was being diverted for a new school! The school system having been installed upstream from the hospital system was now taking priority, and meant that when the water level was low the supply reaching the hospital would be totally inadequate. Following Tjakko's advice and after discussion with the Dzongda; we devised a system to serve both hospital and school and their respective staff quarters in an equitable way.

At the bottom end of the two supply pipes, a common main was then sub-divided and redirected by a distribution grid built inside a concrete chamber fitted with two metal manhole covers, each secured by _two_ padlocks - the key to one padlock held by the school and the key to the other held by the hospital. This meant that the outflow of water could not be altered without a representative from both school and hospital being present. The total quantity of water being supplied to the school or hospital was easily compared and measured by opening a stop cock in each supply line in turn and measuring how many seconds it took to fill a bucket! I have often wondered whether the arrangement has stood the test of time or whether someone has found a way of cheating the system!

For some wives, to have water 'on tap' rather than having to go to a nearby stream was a new experience. Most of the staff quarters including ours were in one long line and being near the far end we found that quite often our water supply dwindled to nothing! When I investigated I discovered the reason; that many of the staff wives having been used to using a mountain stream now thought of their piped water in much the same way! They left their tap turned on full all the time! You could look along the back of the staff quarters and see water gushing out into the drainage channel. To ensure that everyone (especially those toward the end of the pipeline) received their fair share of water, they had to be educated to turn off their taps when the water was not being used.

At certain times of the year the debris in the water was so great that it blocked the small bore pipes that supplied each building. It was a common sight to see the hospital cook armed with a spanner undoing joints in the pipeline to clear blockages. Over time this did not do the plumbing system much good and I wanted to avoid the same treatment being meted out to the new pipe work! Where a pipe had a right angled bend and presented a potential blocking point, it was fitted with a threaded blank, screwed into a T piece, rather than the normal quarter round fitting. This blank could be easily unscrewed to clear a blockage. Again, it would be interesting to know whether this safeguard worked in practice and whether it has helped solve the blockage problems.

Following my frustration with the man who controlled the water system at Kharbandi, and the problems he caused when operating the controls in a drunken state; I found it ironic when the plumber engaged by Yarkey Construction also turned out to be a similar 'thorn in the flesh'. He was a very likable character and showed great willingness to work - when he was sober. His plumbing skill and personal initiative however was strictly limited and he had to be watched like a hawk. The fourteen new toilets serving the new hospital, each had a low level cistern complete with modern plastic diaphragm at the bottom of its bell - a feature that the plumber had never met before! On one of my usual visits to site I was horrified to discover him stripping out the plastic diaphragms and replacing them with crude rubber rings cut from an old lorry inner tube! This is what he had always fitted before - so why change now and use this modern rubbish?

On another occasion; in the renovation of the old hospital ward an alteration was required to the old toilet. The original doorway to this toilet had been bricked up and a new doorway cut through the opposite wall. The site foreman then instructed the plumber to install new piping to reconnect the cistern. At the end of the day on our inspection tour when we reached the re-plumbed toilet, neither of us could believe our eyes or contain our incredulity! The cistern had been reconnected to the water supply sure enough, BUT the plumber had installed the new pipe along the same route as the old one and it was now across the middle of the new door opening! To enter the toilet, you had to either hurdle over the pipe or crawl under it! We stood and laughed ourselves silly, while the bemused plumber looked on at a complete loss to know what we found so funny!

Whilst the work on the hospital was progressing the Japanese were completing the hydroelectric plant in the Tintinbi valley to supply electricity to the nearby town of Zhemgang. It was an education to see them at work for they were the epitome of efficiency. The whole installation down to the last nut and bolt was shipped in from Japan! Even the galvanised electricity poles were imported in sections and bolted together before being concreted into place. In no time, poles appeared all along the road the thirty kilometres to Zhemgang; and almost as soon as I had supplied them with details of my proposed route for the hospital supply, the poles were erected up through the jungle and a mains transformer etc; appeared. So as Phase I of the new hospital neared completion, the revolutionizing mains electricity supply was ready to use! Under the watchful eye of my friend Pema from Kharbandi, two electricians had been busily installing the electrical wiring and fittings in the Phase I buildings; the installation was finished and ready for connection when the mains power came on line. There were no problems and we were able to hand over fully electrified buildings for hospital use when Phase I was complete. This marked a significant step forward for Yebilaptsa.

We did however experience problems of an unexpected nature with the patients when the electrified wards were first used! Each new ward was lit by four fluorescent strips and as many Bhutanese fear both the dark and evil spirits, they thought it was just marvellous that at the flick of a switch they could maintain daylight throughout the night! As the hospital stands in the middle of the jungle it was now a solitary beacon of blazing light visible for miles around. This was no problem humanly speaking (particularly as the government was still working out how electricity should be charged for) but every morning the walls of the wards were plastered with thousands of moths of every size and description imaginable - a lepidopterists paradise! To overcome this unforeseen problem a central night light was installed – its red light visible to humans (and probably evil spirits) but invisible to most other creatures including moths!

Electricity was also installed in the staff quarters for the first time. This required the education of staff wives into the do's and don'ts of using it, and highlighting some of the dangers inherent with electricity and precautions that should be followed. For example - switch off the supply before changing a light bulb and don't do it stood on a wet floor in your bare feet! Use a proper plug to connect an appliance to an electrical socket and don't copy the common practice seen in India, of sticking bare wires into the sockets - held in place with match sticks! Don't replace fuses with thicker and thicker fuse wire to prevent them from blowing! As the purpose of a fuse is to provide a weak point in the circuit that will fail, before the circuit itself is burnt out by overloading!

The approach 'road' to the hospital badly needed upgrading in order to meet the increased usage expected; as up until now it had only been served by an un-metalled track. All road building came under the Indian Army Road Construction Corps which was already working nearby on a new road. Unlike the Japanese who had provided us with electricity for nothing, the Indian Army would do the work – but for a price! Following discussions with their CO we agreed on a price and the road improvement was carried out providing a metalled surface right to the hospital entrance.

The Indian army officers were a friendly crowd and I think it was something of a novelty for them to be working in Bhutan with an English Project Manager. Sadly, the very cordial relations were soured when their senior Officer came to our bungalow immaculately dressed in his best uniform, to deliver a Christmas card. Unfortunately he was met on the doorstep by Jock who had an aversion to anyone carrying anything resembling a stick and we suspected that Jock had at some time been mistreated. The officer carried his swagger stick under the arm and much to our embarrassment and before we were able to intervene, Jock had nipped him hard in the backside, tearing his trousers in the process. The

**Main entrance to the hospital.
Made to resemble the entrance to a Dzong.**

officer's pride was hurt most and though we offered profuse apologies we were sad never to be honoured with another visit!

The new hospital entrance was designed to resemble that of a Dzong and though the pillars and architrave were all constructed of reinforced concrete, skilful plastering and painting made them look as though they were timber. They were beautifully painted by a local man who was extremely skilled in this stylised form of painting seen throughout Bhutan. He painted the entrance with brightly coloured pictures of flowers and animals very much as the entrance to a Dzong might be decorated. It was certainly identifiable by any Bhutanese as the entrance, and from the Matron's Office just inside she could see everyone entering or leaving the hospital! As well as being accessed by either steps or a ramp; directly outside the new entrance was a place where a patient could be easily off-loaded from a vehicle arriving on the newly surfaced road.

Immediately the first phase of building was finished it was handed over for hospital use to relieve pressure on beds and provide badly needed extra medical facilities. The general standard of work and progress made by Yarkey Construction had proved satisfactory in every way so I had no hesitation in awarding them the contracts for Phases II and III. The work continued without a pause, so it was now necessary to screen off the new construction site from the buildings given over to the hospital; so that the new site would not pose a danger to inquisitive patients. The medical staff was also requested not to trespass onto the building site - but human curiosity being what it is; it was a constant struggle deterring them! In the end I arranged a 'conducted tour' with a very informed tour guide to satisfy their curiosity and prevent further incursions!

Many of the Indian workmen at Yebi were Muslim and lived according to a very strict code of conduct with regard to women and alcohol but this did not apply to all the work force - certainly not the plumber! One of the senior construction staff who was Hindu had a 'wife' and baby with him but I was told he also had another wife and family back home. This was his business and not mine as it didn't pose any problem for the Project.

One 'relationship' that did have repercussions for the Project work, reminded me that I was living in a very different culture! A Bhutanese staff member who I knew already had a 'wife' made an 'arrangement' with a young village maiden from Tintinbi who moved in to live with him - a liaison that it seemed had the approval of the girl's family (but not I imagine of the man's wife). Over the two years of the construction programme the inevitable happened and the girl gave birth to their baby. The trade off between the man concerned and the girl's parents, so I learned later, was that a house and shop would be built for her in the village to provide for the future of mother and child. This arrangement only came to light when I made enquiries as to why and where a substantial number of the work force was disappearing from the hospital every Sunday - meant to be their rest day! I discovered they were being employed to build a new house and shop in Tintinbi! As this was not on the hospital site it was outside of my direct control but I strongly suspect that this under cover 'moonlighting' was responsible for a drop in quality of the concrete when we came to build the Operating Theatre Block toward the end of the Project.

Throughout nearly two years of construction the compressive strength of concrete samples had all proved to be well above the acceptable limit; until that is we began work on the Operating Theatre Block when a significant number of samples failed to meet the necessary standard by a large margin. The test results spoke for themselves so Yarkey

Construction had to agree that the pillars should be recast (at their expense of course). By the time the deficiency was discovered the vertical pillars had cured for well over a month and were set rock hard! It meant cutting out the deficient concrete by hand with hammer and cold chisel, whilst leaving the reinforcing rods standing; and for the pillars to then be recast. The work was highly unpopular as you might imagine and involved hard labour for the workers, as well as a delay in payment to the Contractor.

Though I had my suspicion as to why the problem had occurred it could not be proved and my main concern was that the sub-standard work should be rectified. I suspected that cement and other material intended for the Project had been diverted before reaching the hospital for the house and shop being built in the village. I would love to know how Yarkey's quantity surveyor balanced his books after the deficient columns were cut down and recast with new concrete requiring more cement! I did notice that the concrete cut out of the pillars was not wasted but used as hardcore in the floor of the building! After this set-back the building programme continued without any further delay. Having a secure store where desirable material was kept under lock and key, at least the Contractor didn't experience pilfering of building materials - once they had arrived on site!

I did suffer one case of pilfering that caused me some heartache. Following the failure of the slate quarry to produce any more slate after just the one delivery; we had no choice but to use galvanised iron sheeting instead. Though I personally loath the stuff, iron sheeting is seen as a valuable and highly desirable roofing material by many in Bhutan - understandable when people in the south live in leaky thatched houses. As the roof was being constructed by Mandal under my direct supervision, I personally ordered the large quantity of high quality galvanised sheeting required, from a supplier in India. Knowing full well how vulnerable this would be to theft on its way to Yebi, I sent Deepak to travel with the load to ensure its safety but when it arrived he was eight sheets short! Deepak swore that the correct number had been collected from the supplier and he had no idea how or when the missing sheets had been stolen. I now wonder whether they also went toward building the house and shop in Tintinbi - but I will never know for sure! Clearly Deepak was guilty at the very least of neglecting his duty to ensure safe delivery of the order. As he was well paid for what he did I deducted the cost of the missing sheets from his salary and am glad to say there were no further problems.

Partway through the Project I received a 'bombshell' by radio telegram from the Home Ministry in Thimphu in the form of a directive. It ordered me to terminate Deepak's employment immediately stating that he was being expelled from the country - no reason given! I was aware that Bhutanese of Nepali descent were being evicted from Bhutan, either charged with involvement in acts of subversion and terrorism or because they were unable to produce documentary evidence of their right to Bhutanese citizenship. In reality, many like Deepak were simply the innocent victims of an underlying ethnic problem.

The employment of a Counterpart for the Project had been insisted upon by the Royal Government and Deepak's selection had been with full Government approval before TLM had confirmed his appointment. As I'd processed his application and seen his citizenship papers; his school and college reports etc., I knew without doubt that Deepak had been born in Bhutan, his entire education was in Bhutan, and on gaining his Civil Engineering Diploma he had been employed in the Roads Department of the Royal Government of Bhutan. He'd been working continually with me at Yebilaptsa since joining the Project and there was no way he could have been involved in subversive activities which the expulsion order clearly implied. I was absolutely furious that anyone should be treated in such an unjust way in clear violation of his human rights as a citizen of Bhutan - as well as in breach of the Government's Project agreement with TLM.

Being responsible for his appointment in the first place, my first course of action was to raise the matter with the Dzongda in Zhemgang - as he was the King's and the Royal Government's local representative. Whether or not the Dzongda had any prior knowledge of the expulsion order from the Home Ministry, there was no way of knowing but he clearly sensed my agitation over the issue and did his best to placate me. He explained that a replacement for Deepak could and would be found. I pointed out that Deepak had been appointed with the full approval of Government less than two years before and that his knowledge of the Project and his experience in working with me could not be substituted for halfway through the building programme. The Dzongda however was adamant that Deepak had to go. His throw away line which I shall never forget was --

'But we are expelling all Southern Bhutanese from government service!'

There then followed an exchange of messages between myself and the TLM Coordinator in Thimphu, who proved very supportive of my stance. As Head of TLM Bhutan he made direct approaches to the Home Ministry but was unable to make anyone see reason or to change the government decision. As a last resort I drove to Thimphu and discussed the whole matter with the Coordinator in person; who again tried, this time through the Minister for Health to get the Government to reverse its decision. When it remained unmoved, I took the only proper and moral course of action left open to me; and formally notified the Government by letter that if Deepak was expelled I would immediately resign my post as Project Manager and return to Britain – (knowing full well that the Project would come to a standstill and the hospital would remain half finished). It was a form of blackmail - but morally justified blackmail. Under this threat the Government at last relented and gave an undertaking that Deepak could stay. I heaved a sigh of relief and work on the Project resumed.

The last and most complex building of the whole Project was the Operating Theatre and Delivery Suite. This incorporated sluice rooms, changing rooms, showers, a linen store, an anaesthetic room and a recovery room; as well of course as the Operating Theatre and Delivery Room themselves. Throughout the block, the floor and walls up to lintel level were made of polished white marble chip concrete - for ease of cleaning. An electric immersion heater, fed from a tank in the roof provided hot water for scrubbing up even if the incoming supply happened to be blocked! In addition to the mains fluorescent lighting, the OT had additional solar powered emergency lighting, a large south facing skylight and frosted windows front and back; ensuring good light day or night for surgery. Lastly, it had an air conditioning unit to keep it comfortable to work in.

At the same time as this last building was being completed we started to renovate and modify the old original hospital buildings to provide offices and consulting rooms; an upgraded pharmacy; an improved X-ray facility; and an Opthalmistry and Dentistry.

Due to the two year delay in getting the Project started and the effect of inflation, the money pledged for the Project by Germany was now exhausted so the Leprosy Mission had to find another donor to fund a new kitchen and eating area. This money was given by the Channel Islands as a part of their overseas aid. The new kitchen was equipped with the best wood fired stove available from the Swiss workshop in Bumthang and incorporated a special chimney to increase the up-draught – and hopefully carry away smoke effectively - the height of refinement for Bhutan! Food was served through a serving hatch to an adjoining covered eating space; fitted with a bench all round and equipped with a tap and sink for washing off plates - and hopefully hands as well!

In our final tidying up of the site it was necessary to fell a tree that looked as if it might blow down onto the new kitchen. Scattered throughout its branches were some tell-tale structures made of leaves that were home to a particularly aggressive species of ant. These had to be dealt with before the tree could be felled and a courageous labourer skilled in this job was sent up the tree to deal with them. This done, the tree was felled but not quite where intended! Its topmost branch struck the roof of the new kitchen eating area but fortunately missed the adjacent kitchen roof by a whisker; so damage was minimal and soon repaired. The area around the new hospital buildings required landscaping which would involve shifting a considerable volume of soil. Bulldozers were rarer in Bhutan than Snow Leopards but I had spotted one recently parked at the saw mill and Thinley, Yarkey's quartermaster was dispatched post haste to find out if it could be made available. Our mood swung from delight at being told yes; to dismay - when two days later I saw it travelling in the direction of Gelegphu - already some twenty kilometres away. Was this another example of 'yes' meaning 'no' I wondered? Frantic negotiations followed and we managed to secure its immediate return. The machine had been 'well used' and after a couple of days suffered a catastrophic breakdown which could certainly not be fixed with plywood! It was nothing less than a miracle when a second bulldozer appeared out of nowhere and the work was completed!

Looking back at the Yebilaptsa Project I marvel that given my previous lack of experience in civil building it worked out so smoothly. I acknowledge with gratitude, the expertise of so many given to me out of pure goodwill. Without their help the hospital would not have been completed with so little trouble, or to as high a standard as it was. The new enlarged and upgraded hospital would hopefully provide vastly improved medical facilities and meet the health care needs of thousands of people in a large area of Central Bhutan, for many years to come.

My workload in seeing the Project through to its successful completion over the three years had been considerable. Usually, every day for six days a week I had worked from early morning until well after the building work on site had finished for the day, in often demanding physical conditions in heat and humidity. Toward the end of the Project I began to show signs of fatigue and suffered several dizzy spells whilst walking round the site. Then I developed a persistent cough that would not respond to treatment. As all the new buildings were finished and the renovation work on the old buildings was also complete, Dorothy and I decided to return home to Britain slightly earlier than planned. So in April of 1994 we left Yebilaptsa for home, leaving some final fitting out work for Deepak to oversee. It was especially hard to say goodbye to our carpenter and good friend Mandal for whom Dorothy and I had developed the greatest respect and affection during our two years at Yebi. Jock also loved Mandal and we were able to leave him in Mandal's care, knowing they would both be very happy to share life together.

The completed hospital buildings at Yebilaptsa

Our premature departure meant that we missed the official hand over of the new hospital to the Royal Government. When we arrived home a chest X-ray revealed that both lungs were full of a serious bacterial infection but after treatment and rest, I soon returned to full health and strength. I was still employed by the Leprosy Mission and thanks to the marvels of modern communication was able to complete and send drawings out to Deepak by Fax, via Thimphu. To assist in the upkeep of the hospital in future and hopefully ensure that things would continue to work; I also compiled a maintenance manual dealing with topics like the frequency with which septic tanks should be emptied; the best way to clear blockages in water pipes; the upkeep of toilets; replacing of fuses; etc. etc..

My last visit to Bhutan was nine months later in January 1995 to carry out a final inspection of the Hospital. This is standard practice to ensure that no serious faults or major defects in the structure have developed as it settled; before paying over the final 2% of the contract price to Yarkey Construction and closing the Project bank account. The Royal Government granted me a two week visa to complete my work!

Together with the work force at the end of the Project!

Due to circumstances beyond my control, the plane arrived one day late; I spent a further day in Thimphu obtaining the necessary permit to allow me to travel to Yebilaptsa; then two days driving to Yebi and back used four more days in total of my precious allotted two weeks. One further day was taken up travelling to Gelegphu and back to close the Project bank account; and the last scheduled flight that I could take out of Bhutan was the day before my visa actually expired! That left just six days to carry out the inspection; meet and pay off the contractor; and say goodbye for the last time to the staff at Yebilaptsa and my other friends in Bhutan! It was not at all the way I would have liked to bid farewell to those who had become friends and colleagues of several years standing and who I might never see again; or to take my leave of the country that had been home for six full and fascinating years and which held so many memories for me!

During the twenty years since I was last at Yebilaptsa I'd often wondered how the hospital was standing up to wear and tear and the test of time. Also, whether if I did manage to revisit Bhutan I might be disappointed when I saw what the hospital now looked like. During 2015, I discovered much to my amazement that I could view the front of Yebi hospital from ground level on my computer thanks to the 'Google Earth' app.; and was delighted to discover that it looks beautifully cared for; is planted around with trees; was freshly painted; and looked on the outside at least, unscathed by earth tremors. If you want to look for yourself, find Zhemgang, Bhutan, and go a little further south until you're looking down on a small group of buildings surrounded by the forest and you will probably have found Yebilaptsa Hospital!

I believe there are two main lessons to be learned from the Yebilaptsa Project which are generally applicable to other such development projects; factors that I believe led to its successful completion.

Firstly: Providing **(1)** a full specification for the structure and **(2)** a legally binding contract; ensured that the work was carried out to as high a standard as the contractor was capable; and the Project was successfully completed without undue dispute or delay.

Secondly:

Major corruption was discouraged by maintaining a direct and strict financial control of project expenditure 'at site'; whilst at the same time a fair system of payment to the contractor based on work done, meant that the momentum of the Hospital construction programme was effectively maintained throughout.

Acknowledgements

I would like to acknowledge the important contributions made to the Yebilaptsa Hospital Project by the following people.

Rob Fielding - for his overall design concept and for his initial work in planning and preparing for the eventual hospital construction.

Pema Geyltshen for designing and overseeing the electrification of the hospital.

Tjakko Haaijer who advised in the design of the new hospital water supply system.

Praffula Mandal for his loyalty, cheerfulness and unstinting hard work on the Project.

Doug Le Mesurier who helped and encouraged me in many important respects.

Reflections

Working in Bhutan changed my outlook on life in so many ways – in living among a people who still held dear to many values that in the West have been greatly eroded in our pursuit of material gain. I know I've been enriched through living in such a different society which still valued strong family ties; courtesy in one's dealing with people; a respect for one's elders; and satisfaction with a simple basic way of life.

It was particularly rewarding to be in Bhutan near the start of its development process; when the way of life for the majority of its people had remained unchanged for many centuries. Just a few years before I first went there; there were no roads, no electricity, and no communication links with the outside world. For the vast majority of Bhutan's people their only water supply was what the streams and rivers delivered naturally. Their houses had no glass to keep out draughts, no chimneys to take away smoke, no damp course to stop the penetration of water; and no 'mod cons' such as bathrooms or toilets. When I first went to work in Bhutan in 1984, according to UN statistics based on the comparative Gross National Product's (GNP) of countries; Bhutan was ranked as one of the poorest nations on earth. This was somewhat misleading as most Bhutanese were subsistence farmers and trading links with the outside world were almost non-existent, so Bhutan had no 'gross national product'. Having said this, the general standard of living was undoubtedly very poor. I can hardly write a book about Bhutan without including the former King's riposte when asked by a reporter about Bhutan's Gross National Product or lack of it - to which he famously replied that he was more concerned with his peoples Gross National Happiness!

Electricity was unknown in Bhutan before the first small hydroelectric plants were built there in the early 1970's! In 1987 the much larger 320 Megawatt plant at Chukha was completed, which I had been able to visit with my students several times during its construction. An even larger plant has now been built lower on the same river at Tala, with an output of 1020 Megawatts. More major hydroelectric plants are already under construction and planned including one near Yebilaptsa; mainly to provide India with the power it so desperately needs to help fuel its own future development. Only a tiny fraction of their combined output meets all the electrical energy needs of Bhutan! Under a joint agreement India builds and maintains these plants and pays Bhutan for the power India receives as a result. As electricity is made more widely available in Bhutan it will bring welcome light and heat during the dark cold winters especially to people in the north of the country but it will also inevitably lead to a desire for the peripheral aids that electricity makes possible - the fridge, vacuum cleaner, and of course television!

The ban on television in Bhutan was lifted as recently as June 1999! I suppose when you see TV for the first time it seems such a miracle of science and communication that people naturally want to watch it and aspire to owning a set of their own. That TV exercises a powerful and all too often corrosive influence on attitudes, moral standards and personal and social conduct only becomes apparent after years of exposure. After having been isolated and protected from the influence of the rest of the world for centuries; how the sudden exposure of the Bhutanese to TV will impact on their national social psyche and culture in the long term, remains to be seen! In these early days of TV in Bhutan, broadcasts are being carefully controlled by the government.

Bhutan became the first country in the world to ban smoking in all public spaces when it passed its Tobacco Control Act in June 2010.

A microwave telecommunications system was installed by the Japanese throughout Bhutan and completed in 1994. It even reaches to Yebilaptsa but unfortunately it came too late for us as we had just returned home! Bhutan is now independently linked by satellite to the rest of the world and is joined to the World Wide Web. It has Internet Cafes in Thimphu and some of its citizens have e-mail addresses! Through these marvels of modern communication I am able to keep in touch with what is happening there today. Certainly Thimphu has grown out of all recognition in these past twenty years and its main street is now lined with multi-story buildings in place of the simple traditional one and two story shops that I knew.

Thankfully the rest of Bhutan is developing at a rather slower rate but the process of change is touching the lives of Bhutanese even in the remotest corners of the Kingdom. Many small development projects have made a real difference to the living standards of people across Bhutan; with the provision of good things like toilets, piped water supplies and improvements in the building of the traditional houses; the planting of orchards; the introduction of potato growing; improving rice strains; bee keeping for honey production; and dairy farming to produce milk and cheese – to name but a few.

Bhutan has advanced such a long way in terms of its development in a very short time and credit is due to the foresight and wisdom of its rulers for the way in which the general standard of living has been improved for many of its people. That development process is still ongoing as the government seeks the right way forward which will best serve its people but without sacrificing Bhutan's unique identity.

In 2015 I was able to 'visit' the hospital at Yebilaptsa again; sadly, not in person but via the 'Google Earth' web-site and to my surprise I was able to view the front of the hospital from ground level! To see it in this way and know that one of their special recording cameras has visited this formerly remote spot; indicates to me how far Bhutan has moved into the modern era since I was last there just twenty years ago, when Yebilaptsa Hospital wasn't even on the telephone!

To have worked in Bhutan during these early formative years of change was especially fascinating. It brought home to me how development inevitably alters a society - both for good and ill; and how in the course of development long held traditions and culture may be challenged and even unwittingly be eroded. Bhutan is still coming to terms with so much change in such a short time, and it remains to be seen how it will cope as a nation with the shift in the thinking and traditionally held views of its people which will inevitably come with its increased exposure to the outside world. If only somehow we could bring to people the most desirable and essential improvements to their standard of living like clean water, proper sanitation, basic education, widely available health care, and even electricity; without at the same time importing our western values that puts so much emphasis upon what one has, rather than what one is; and what one can get, rather than what one can give!

Bhutan is not perfect and is certainly not the Shangri la that visitors sometimes make it out to be. The development of any country after all, is not just about improving the infrastructure; about building roads, establishing communication links, providing for the proper health care and education of its people - though all of these things are of course important. Development should also involve a process of 'democratisation' in its widest sense. It is about recognition of individual human rights whatever your ethnic origin; about improving the legal system to provide true justice for all no matter what your station in life; about freedom of speech and of worship without fear of persecution. Such ideals take longer to achieve and in some of these areas, Bhutan still has a way to go.

Very recently major changes in the political structure and government of the country have taken place. King Jigme Singye Wangchuk who ruled Bhutan throughout my time there has now abdicated in favour of his eldest son. The coronation of the new King, Jigme Khesar Namgyal Wangchuk took place in early 2009. Also in 2009 Bhutan held its first democratic elections on a one person one vote basis; and the structure and exercise of government at both national and local level have changed to reflect that process of democratisation. Dawa Gyaltshen, who was a former colleague and my friend at Kharbandi, was elected to the National Assembly to represent his home district in 2012. I was thrilled to learn that on July 20th 2015 the Prime Minister submitted a recommendation to the new King to appoint Dawa the 'Minister for Home and Cultural Affairs', so he is now addressed as Lyonpo Dawa Gyaltshen and wears an orange scarf.

My other good friend Pema Gyeltshen who has kept me regularly in touch with Bhutan by e-mail, shared with me recently that his wife had just had a gallstone removed successfully by keyhole surgery and he had been able to watch the process on a screen outside the operating theatre – at Gidakom Hospital of all places! Only twenty years ago performing such an operation anywhere in Bhutan would have been beyond ones wildest imagination.

There are now no less than four airstrips in the country rather than just the one in Paro that served the whole of Bhutan when I was there! Many roads have been greatly improved and many more built. Although so much change has taken place and the infrastructure of Bhutan has developed almost beyond recognition since I lived there last, it is still a beautiful and largely unspoilt country. It is because the forest and jungle survives largely intact, that animals and birds continue to live here that have long since disappeared from former strongholds elsewhere in the Himalayas. My hope is, that the current stance of the Royal Government to conserve and protect its flora and fauna will be maintained, so that the abundant and in some cases unique plants and animals of Bhutan to be found in this largely un-spoilt corner of our world, may continue to be conserved for many years to come; even if it means continued restriction of tourist numbers and their access to certain areas of the country. These natural habitats have survived up until now because they have remained out of the grasp of modern man!

Before anyone contemplates leaving home to live and work

for several years in a society so radically different to their own, they should realise that their experience will be more than an adventure, it will be life changing - they will never be the same person again. One's exposure to another culture and to life outside the 'comfort zone', mean that when you return to 'normality' you may well be somewhat estranged from those many people who prefer to live cocooned in the so called security of materialism and the creature comforts of our western way of life. They will discover that many at home do not really want to know how the other two thirds of the world live. Some may show polite interest to a limited degree, but you will have to keep reminding yourself that they have not experienced the kind of situations that you have; and being honest, your own attitude was probably much the same as theirs anyway, before you left to work in foreign parts.

On your return home you can soon find yourself living a schizophrenic life with a foot in both worlds, as it were. All too soon you can take things like clean water on tap, proper sanitation and a reliable electricity supply for granted, just as you did before. All too soon you can find yourself grumbling about the difficulty of getting an appointment to see your doctor; the deterioration of public services; the constant bickering of politicians; and the cost of living - putting to the back of your mind that many in our world have no access to proper medical care, no public services, no democratic rights and face a constant struggle just to stay alive.

When I finally returned to live in Britain in 1994 after spending six years in Bhutan, I found Britain had also changed while I'd been away. It appeared to me as if people knew and cared even less about their immediate neighbours than they had when I left in 1984. We seemed as a nation to be progressively losing touch with core basic human values such as a respect and care for one another and a concern for the most needy and vulnerable in our society. Our politicians seemed far more preoccupied with the national economy than in provision for the sick and the elderly. They were certainly not concerned with Britain's **Gross National Happiness** but very much more about its **Gross National Product**! There were more homeless people sleeping in shop doorways in our major cities. Drug addiction had escalated. The work ethic for many had been replaced by a culture of leisure; and there seemed a prevailing attitude of living the good life for today and not bothering oneself too much about tomorrow. Law and order were becoming more of a concern, especially violence - be it mugging, rape or threatening behaviour. Alcohol abuse and dependency was on the increase especially among the younger generation. The question that kept pursuing me was 'Where are *WE* heading as a society'? Was my perception of life in Britain a knee jerk reaction to having been away for several years and in particular to having lived in Bhutan?

It was impossible for me not to compare the two societies. British society - increasingly rich in things and lacking in care; Bhutan - materialistically lacking but upholding strong family ties, care of the elderly, concern for one's neighbours and an acceptance of the need to work in order to feed and support one's family - as well as to have some time to enjoy simple pastimes. There were no homeless in Bhutan. No drug addiction that I knew of. Not a lot of crime. It was not a perfect society by any means but it challenged our western attitudes and lifestyle in so many ways. My time in Bhutan brought home to me the importance of re-establishing in Britain these basic core human values that encourage compassion and care in society; dare I add, even at the expense of some of the trappings of our 21st century consumer orientated way of life!

I became a Christian in my teens and my Christian belief was in part instrumental in taking me to Bhutan. But before being accepted to work in what is a very Buddhist country I had to give an undertaking not to proselytise - that is actively attempt to convert others to my faith, as there is not yet the freedom of religious belief and expression in Bhutan that we uphold in Britain. What I believe as a Christian was an important motivating force in my going to work in Bhutan and though that work was primarily concerned with development, I would hope that what I did and the way I did it would in itself be testament to the Christian values and faith I hold to. I was not persuaded to convert to Tibetan Buddhism - the religion held by the great majority of Bhutanese. However, I found so much to be admired in the quiet nature and caring attitude of my Bhutanese colleagues and neighbours throughout my six years in Bhutan - both the Buddhists and the Christians, who I remember with great affection.

To have had the opportunity to work alongside and share in the lives of such delightful, gentle, hospitable and courteous people; to have seen something of Bhutan's largely unspoilt and magnificent scenery; to have had - albeit tantalising glimpses of its wildlife; and to have witnessed the emergence of Bhutan into the 20th century whilst it still retained much of its age old tradition, art, crafts and culture; was an experience that I will always remember and cherish. It is my hope that this account has conveyed to you something of the uniqueness of this tiny Himalayan Kingdom and its people. As I reflect upon my

SIX YEARS IN BHUTAN I realise the privilege that was mine.

Traditional Bhutanese Mural

This traditional painting on the wall of a house, depicts how an elephant, a monkey, a hare and a peacock - cooperated together in order to reach the fruit of the tree. This same mural design has been painted on the walls of houses in Bhutan for centuries and its allegorical symbolism conveys a vitally important message for us all in the 21st century. Whether we live in Bhutan or Britain we need to cooperate with one another if we are to achieve the very best for all.

A fully illustrated copy of 'SIX YEARS in BHUTAN' with photographs in full colour; together with a substantial additional gallery of colour photographs depicting the landscape, people, architecture and everyday life in BHUTAN, all on a CD-Rom in pdf format for the computer; can be obtained by writing to antiqueland@hotmail.co.uk when full details/cost will be provided.

**If you enjoyed reading
'SIX YEARS in BHUTAN'
then please recommend it to your
family and friends.**

Your recommendation is the
 books best publicity.

If you would like to comment on
the book then please send
your feed-back to
johnstedman@uwclub.net

A positive comment and star rating
on the **Amazon** or **Kindle** web-site
would also be much appreciated,
but only if **you** feel the book
merits one.

Glossary of Dzongkha (Bhutanese) Words

ara - common alcoholic drink

bangchhang - home-brewed wine usually served warm
bangchung - round basket made of bamboo with interlocking lid used to contain food
bukhari - wood burning stove

chhang - or bangchhang - a home-brewed alcoholic beer or wine made from cereals
chorten - a religious monument often containing a Buddhist artefact
chhu - river or water
chetrum - Bhutanese unit of currency. 100 chetrums = one ngultrum
chugo - hard lozenge of yak cheese for chewing – normally bought on a string

dasho - senior government officer
doma - chew consisting of areca nut with lime - wrapped in a betel leaf
datsi - traditional soft small round cheese
Driglam Namzha - Bhutanese Royal Etiquette
druk - dragon
Drukpa - followers of religious school of the Drukpa Kagyudpa
drukpa - citizens of Bhutan
Druk Yul - Bhutanese name for Bhutan meaning - Thunder Dragon Kingdom
Druk Gyalpo - name given to the King meaning - Precious Ruler of the Dragon Kingdom
dzong - administrative, judicial and religious regional centre
dzongda - administrative head of the Dzong traditionally appointed by the King
Dzongkhang - district

dzongkha - national language of Bhutan – literally the language(kha) of the Dzong

geylong - young monk
goemba - or gompa, a temple or monastery
gozozampo - Bhutanese greeting meaning "how do you do!"
gup - village head man

kabne - man's ceremonial scarf worn on official occasions– compulsory in a Dzong
kadrinche - expression of thanks meaning "thank you".
kho (or Buko) - traditional garment worn by a male – often beautifully hand woven
kira - traditional garment worn by a female – also hand woven
Khenkha - language spoken in a region of Central Southern Bhutan
kukri - a Nepali Gurkha knife with a short but wide curved blade

la - a mark of respect used at the end of a word or sentence
La - mountain pass
lama - monk
lhakhang - temple
Lyonpo - Minister in charge of a Government Department who wears an orange scarf
mandala - cosmic diagram seen in Dzongs and temples and used for instruction
mani wall - wall inscribed with the Buddhist mantra along both sides
momo - small meat (usually pork) filled steamed dumpling

ngultrum - Bhutanese unit of currency

puja - religious ritual carried out by a lama or lamas

raichu - ceremonial scarf worn by women – compulsory when in a Dzong

240

singchhang - fermented drink usually drunk cold

sharchopkha - language spoken in eastern Bhutan

suja - butter tea – the greasy tea containing salt and butter served in Bhutan

Taktsang - "Tigers Nest" Bhutan's most famous monastery - situated in Paro valley

thanka - Religious banner usually displayed only at a yearly religious festival

Tashicho Dzong - Dzong in Thimphu where the King and his chief ministers are based

Tshogdu - the National Assembly

yak - large shaggy haired cattle that live at high altitude in the Himalaya

63457015R00138

Made in the USA
Charleston, SC
05 November 2016